MW01055255

Helping Students Understand Geometry

By
BARBARA SANDALL, Ed.D., and MELFRIED OLSON, Ed.D.

COPYRIGHT © 2005 Mark Twain Media, Inc.

ISBN 10-digit: 1-58037-302-X
13-digit: 978-1-58037-302-9

Printing No. CD-404029

Mark Twain Media, Inc., Publishers
Distributed by Carson-Dellosa Publishing LLC

Visit us at www.carsondellosa.com

The purchase of this book entitles the buyer to reproduce the student pages for classroom use only. Other permissions may be obtained by writing Mark Twain Media, Inc., Publishers.

All rights reserved. Printed in the United States of America.

Table of Contents

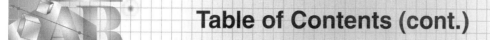

Table of Contents (cont.)

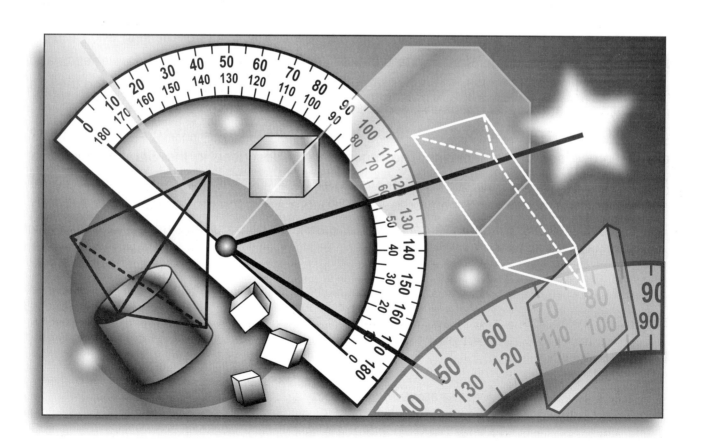

Introduction

The *Helping Students Understand Math Series* will introduce students in middle school through high school to the topics of Pre-Algebra, Algebra I, Algebra II, and Geometry. All of the worktexts will be aligned with the National Council of Teachers of Mathematics (NCTM) *Principles and Standards for School Mathematics.*

This series is written for classroom teachers, parents, families, and students. The worktexts in this series can be used as a full unit of study or as individual lessons to supplement textbooks or curriculum programs. Parents and students can use this series as an enhancement to what is being done in the classroom or as a tutorial at home. All students will benefit from these activities, but the series was designed with the struggling math student in mind. The **concepts** and **explanations for the concepts** are described in simple **step-by-step instructions** with **examples** in the introduction of each lesson. Students will be given practice problems using the concepts introduced and descriptions of real-life applications of the concepts.

According to the Mathematics Education Trust and the NCTM, new technologies require that the fundamentals of algebra and algebraic thinking should be a part of the background for all citizens. These technologies also provide opportunities to generate numerical examples, graph data, analyze patterns, and make generalizations. An understanding of algebra is also important because business and industry require higher levels of thinking and problem solving. NCTM also suggests that understanding geometry, including the characteristics and properties of two- and three-dimensional shapes, spatial relationships, symmetry, and the use of visualization and spatial reasoning, can also be used in solving problems.

NCTM *Standards* suggest content and vocabulary are necessary, but of equal importance are the processes of mathematics. The process skills described in the *Standards* include: problem solving, reasoning, communication, and connections. The worktexts in the series will address both the content and the processes of algebra and geometry and algebraic thinking. This worktext, *Helping Students Understand Geometry,* will help students understand the basic concepts of geometry.

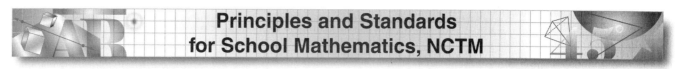

Principles and Standards for School Mathematics, NCTM

Number and Operations
Students will be enabled to:
- Understand numbers, ways of representing numbers, relationships among numbers, and number systems.
- Understand meanings of operations and how they relate to one another.
- Compute fluently and make reasonable estimates.

Algebra
Students will be enabled to:
- Understand patterns, relations, and functions.
- Represent and analyze mathematical situations and structures using algebraic symbols.
- Use mathematical models to represent and understand quantitative relationships.
- Analyze change in various contexts.

Geometry
Students will be enabled to:
- Analyze characteristics and properties of two- and three-dimensional geometric shapes and develop mathematical arguments about geometric relationships.
- Specify locations and describe spatial relationships using coordinate geometry and other representational systems.
- Apply transformations and use symmetry to analyze mathematical situations.
- Use visualization, spatial reasoning, and geometric modeling to solve problems.

Measurement
Students will be enabled to:
- Understand measurable attributes of objects and the units, systems, and processes of measurement.
- Apply appropriate techniques, tools, and formulas to determine measurements.

Data Analysis and Probability
Students will be enabled to:
- Formulate questions that can be addressed with data and collect, organize, and display relevant data to answer them.
- Select and use appropriate statistical methods to analyze data.
- Develop and evaluate inferences and predictions that are based on data.
- Understand and apply basic concepts of probability.

NCTM Standards and Expectations
Grades 6–12 Geometry, NCTM

Analyze characteristics and properties of two- and three-dimensional geometric shapes and develop mathematical arguments about geometric relationships

Expectations Grades 6–8

- Precisely describe, classify, and understand relationships among types of two- and three-dimensional objects using their defining properties;
- Understand relationships among the angles, side lengths, perimeters, areas, and volumes of similar objects;
- Create and critique inductive and deductive arguments concerning geometric ideas and relationships, such as congruence, similarity, and the Pythagorean relationship.

Expectations Grades 9–12:

- Analyze properties and determine attributes of two- and three-dimensional objects;
- Explore relationships (including congruence and similarity) among classes of two- and three-dimensional geometric objects, make and test conjectures about them, and solve problems involving them;
- Establish the validity of geometric conjectures using deduction, prove theorems, and critique arguments made by others;
- Use trigonometric relationships to determine lengths and angle measures.

Specify locations and describe spatial relationships using coordinate geometry and other representational systems

Expectations Grades 6–8:

- Use coordinate geometry to represent and examine the properties of geometric shapes;
- Use coordinate geometry to examine special geometric shapes, such as regular polygons or those with pairs of parallel or perpendicular sides.

Expectations Grades 9–12:

- Use Cartesian coordinates and other coordinate systems, such as navigational, polar, or spherical systems, to analyze geometric situations;
- Investigate conjectures and solve problems involving two- and three-dimensional objects represented with Cartesian coordinates.

Apply transformations and use symmetry to analyze mathematical situations

Expectations Grades 6–8:

- Describe sizes, positions, and orientations of shapes under informal transformations such as flips, turns, slides, and scaling;
- Examine the congruence, similarity, and line or rotational symmetry of objects using transformations.

NCTM Standards and Expectations Grades 6–12 Geometry, NCTM (cont.)

Expectations Grades 9–12:

- Understand and represent translations, reflections, rotations, and dilations of objects in the plane by using sketches, coordinates, vectors, function notation, and matrices;
- Use various representations to help understand the effects of simple transformations and their compositions.

Use visualization, spatial reasoning, and geometric modeling to solve problems

Expectations Grades 6–8:

- Draw geometric objects with specified properties, such as side lengths or angle measures;
- Use two-dimensional representations of three-dimensional objects to visualize and solve problems such as those involving surface area and volume;
- Use visual tools such as networks to represent and solve problems;
- Use geometric models to represent and explain numerical and algebraic relationships;
- Recognize and apply geometric ideas and relationships in areas outside the mathematics classroom, such as art, science, and everyday life.

Expectations Grades 9–12:

- Draw and construct representations of two- and three-dimensional geometric objects using a variety of tools;
- Visualize three-dimensional objects and spaces from different perspectives and analyze their cross sections;
- Use vertex-edge graphs to model and solve problems;
- Use geometric models to gain insights into, and answer questions in, other areas of mathematics;
- Use geometric ideas to solve problems in, and gain insights into, other disciplines and other areas of interest such as art and architecture.

Common Mathematics/Geometry Symbols and Terms

Term	Symbol/Definition	Example
Undefined Terms	Cannot be defined but can be described	Point
Point	Specific place in space. It has no dimension, length, width, or depth. It is represented by a dot and labeled by a single capital letter.	● A Point A
Line	Set of continuous points that extend indefinitely in either direction	 Line *AB*, *AC*, or *BC* Also written $\overleftrightarrow{AB}$, $\overleftrightarrow{AC}$, $\overleftrightarrow{BC}$
Plane	Flat surface that extends infinitely in all directions; when a plane is represented by a four-sided figure, place a capital letter in one of the corners of its representation to label it.	
Line Segment	A line segment is part of a line with two endpoints. Two letters with a bar over them represent the line segment.	 Segment *AB*, or written $\overline{AB}$
Ray	A ray has one endpoint and extends infinitely in the opposite direction from the endpoint. Rays are identified with arrows on top of the letters showing both the endpoint and the direction in which the rays are going.	 Ray *AC* or *BC* Also written $\overrightarrow{AC}$, $\overrightarrow{BC}$
Opposite Rays	Two rays traveling in opposite directions that have the same endpoint and form a straight line	 Rays BA and BC are opposite rays. Also written $\overleftarrow{BA}$, $\overrightarrow{BC}$

Common Mathematics/Geometry Symbols and Terms (cont.)

Term	Symbol/Definition	Example
Parallel Lines	Two lines in the same plane that do not intersect Symbol: ‖	 AB ‖ BC
Collinear	Points that lie on the same line	 A, B, and C are collinear.
Non-Collinear Points	Points that do not lie on the same line	 A, B, D, and E are non-collinear because they cannot all lie on the same line simultaneously.
Angle	A pair of two rays that have the same endpoint; the rays are the sides of the angle	
Vertex of an Angle	The point where the rays meet is the vertex of the angle.	 Vertex
Polygon	Closed-sided figure with three or more sides that intersect only at their endpoints. The sides of the polygons are line segments. The points where the sides intersect are called the **vertices** of the polygons.	

Common Mathematics/Geometry Symbols and Terms (cont.)

Term	Symbol/Definition	Example
Congruent Shapes	Two shapes are congruent if they have exactly the same size and shape.	
Perimeter of a Polygon	The sum of the measures of all of the sides, expressed in linear units such as inches, feet, meters, centimeters, miles, etc.	If each side is 1 cm, then the perimeter is 4 cm.
Area	The number of square units the figure contains, expressed in square inches, square centimeters, etc.	If each side is 1 cm, then the area is side x side, so the area is $1 \times 1 = 1 \text{ cm}^2$.
Ratio	The quotient when one number is divided by another number; mostly written in fraction form	If the numbers are represented by a and b, then the ratio of the two numbers is $\frac{a}{b}$, or a divided by b as long as $b \neq 0$.
Proportion	An equation that sets two ratios equal	$\frac{a}{b} = \frac{c}{d}$
Postulate	A generalization that cannot be proven true; it is just accepted as true	Two points determine a single line. Three non-collinear points not on the same line are needed to determine a single plane. If two planes intersect, they intersect in exactly one line.

Common Mathematics/Geometry Symbols and Terms (cont.)

Term	Symbol/Definition	Example
Theorem	A generalization that can be proven true	If two lines intersect, then they intersect at exactly one point.
		Through a line and a point not on that line, there is only one plane.
Geometric Proofs	A proof is an organized series of statements that show the statement to be proved follows logically from known facts. Facts are given statements, postulates, and previously proven theorems. The first goal of writing proofs is to convince yourself that the statement is true. The second is to write them in a way that would convince a reader.	Inductive reasoning starts with examples, and then the examples are used to generate conjectures. Deductive reasoning is reasoning that uses definitions, theorems, and postulates to prove a new theorem true. In deductive proofs, compare the statements with the reasons. In deductive proofs, ask yourself: What do you know? What can you infer? What can you conclude?
Addition Sign	+	$2 + 2 = 4$
Subtraction Sign	$-$	$4 - 2 = 2$
Multiplication Sign	x or a dot • or a number and a letter(s) together or parentheses	3×2 $2 \cdot 2$ $2x$ $2(2)$
Division Sign	÷ or a slash mark (/) or a horizontal fraction bar, or $\sqrt{}$	$6 \div 2$ $4/2$ $\frac{4}{2}$ $2\overline{)4}$

Common Mathematics/Geometry Symbols and Terms (cont.)

Term	Symbol/Definition	Example
Equals or is equal to	$=$	$2 + 2 = 4$
Does Not Equal	$\neq$	$5 \neq 1$
Less than	$<$	$2 < 4$
Greater than	$>$	$4 > 2$
Greater than or equal to	$\geq$	$2 + 3 \geq 4$
Less than or equal to	$\leq$	$2 + 1 \leq 4$
Congruent	$\cong$	$\triangle ABC \cong \triangle DEF$
Perpendicular	$\perp$	Line segment *AB* is perpendicular to line segment *CD* or written as $\overline{AB} \perp \overline{CD}$.
Pi	A number that is approximately $\frac{22}{7}$ or 3.14, represented as π	3.1415926...
Similar	$\sim$	$\triangle ABC \sim \triangle DEF$
Arc	Part of a circle	Arc *AB* or written as $\overset{\frown}{AB}$
Square	Quadrilateral with four equal sides and four right angles	
Rectangle	A parallelogram that has four right angles	
Parallelogram	Quadrilateral whose opposite sides are parallel	
Quadrilateral	Polygon with four sides	

Common Mathematics/Geometry Symbols and Terms (cont.)

Term	Symbol/Definition	Example
Pentagon	Polygon with five sides	
Hexagon	Polygon with six sides	
Octagon	Polygon with eight sides	
Coordinates/ Coordinate Plane	Coordinates on a line are points that can be matched one-to-one with real numbers. The number is matched with a coordinate. A coordinate plane is a grid that can be used for graphing. Numbers can be matched one-to-one with ordered pairs of numbers. The horizontal line is called the *x*-axis, and the vertical line that is perpendicular to the *x*-axis is called the *y*-axis.	
Ordered Pairs	Describes a point on a graph. The first number in the pair tells the location on the *x*-axis. The second number tells the location on the *y*-axis.	(3, 8) means 3 to the right of 0 on the *x*-axis and 8 up on the *y*-axis. The point is where these two numbers intersect.
Midpoint	The midpoint of a line segment is the single point that is an equal distance from both endpoints.	The midpoint of a line segment is $\left(\frac{x_1 + x_2}{2}, \frac{y_1 + y_2}{2}\right)$

Common Mathematics/Geometry Symbols and Terms (cont.)

Term	Symbol/Definition	Example
Linear Equation	$ax + by = c$, where a, b, and c are constants, and x and y are variables.	$ax + by = c$
Angle Bisector	A ray that bisects the angle	
Obtuse Angle	An angle that is greater than 90°	
Acute Angle	An angle that is less than 90°	
Right Angle	An angle that is equal to 90°	
Vertical Angle	Four angles are formed when two lines intersect. The opposite angles always have the same measure, and they are called vertical angles.	
Supplementary Angles	If two angles form a straight line, the sum of the two angles is 180°.	
Complementary Angles	When the sum of two angles is 90°	
Adjacent Angles	Angles that share a common side	∠ABD is adjacent to ∠DBC

Common Mathematics/Geometry Symbols and Terms (cont.)

Term	Symbol/Definition	Example
Reflex Angle	A reflex angle is greater than 180° but less than 360°. The arc at the vertex indicates that it is a reflex angle.	
Straight Angle	Forms a straight line	
Protractor	Tool used to measure angles	
Symmetry	If a figure can be divided into two parts, each of which is a mirror image of the other, then it has line symmetry, or reflection symmetry.	
Equation	Mathematical sentence in which two phrases are connected with an equals (=) sign	$5 + 7 = 12$ $3x = 12$ $1 = 1$
Absolute Value	The absolute value of a number can be considered as the distance between the number and zero on a number line. The absolute value of every number will be either positive or zero. Real numbers come in paired opposites, a and $-a$, that are the same distance from the origin but in opposite directions.	Absolute value of a: $|a| = a$ if a is positive $|a| = a$ if a is negative $|a| = 0$ if $a = 0$ If 0 is the origin on the number line to the left, then 3 is the absolute value of the pair -3 and +3, because they are both 3 marks from 0.
Circumference	The distance around a circle	$C = \pi d$ $C = \pi 2r$ d = diameter; r = radius

Common Mathematics/Geometry Symbols and Terms (cont.)

Term	Symbol/Definition	Example
Diameter	The measurement of a straight line passing through the center of a circle, or 2 x radius (2*r*)	The diameter (*d*) of this circle is 4 cm.
Radius	One-half the diameter of a circle, or $\frac{1}{2}$ x diameter ($\frac{1}{2}d$)	The radius (*r*) of this circle is 2 cm.
Area of a Circle	The measure of the interior of a circle	$A = \pi r^2$ $A = \pi\left(\dfrac{d}{2}\right)^2$ *d* = diameter; *r* = radius
Distance	The length of a line segment; given two points in a plane, (x_1, y_1) and (x_2, y_2), the distance between them is given by the formula: $\sqrt{(x_1 - x_2)^2 + (y_1 - y_2)^2}$	Given the points: (-2, 3) and (3, 1), the distance is $\sqrt{(\text{-}2 - 3)^2 + (3 - 1)^2} =$ $\sqrt{25 + 4} = \sqrt{29}$
Slope	The measure of the incline of a line	To find slope: Slope intercept $3x + y - 2 = 0$ Solve for *y* : $y = \text{-}3x + 2$ The number in front of the *x* (-3) is the slope; the 2 is the *y*-intercept. Two-Point Method: Slope $= \dfrac{y_2 - y_1}{x_2 - x_1}$ Given two points on the line: (3, 2) and (5, 1) Slope $= \dfrac{1 - 2}{5 - 3} = \dfrac{\text{-}1}{2}$

Common Mathematics/Geometry Symbols and Terms (cont.)

Term	Symbol/Definition	Example
Triangle	A three-sided polygon	Δ ABC
Isosceles Triangle	A triangle that has two congruent angles and two congruent sides	
Equilateral Triangle	A triangle that has three equal sides (and angles)	
Acute Triangle	A triangle in which every angle is less than 90°	
Obtuse Triangle	A triangle in which one angle is greater than 90°	
Right Triangle	A triangle in which one angle is equal to 90°	90°
Equiangular Triangle	A triangle in which all angles (and sides) are equal; same as equilateral triangle	60° 60° 60°
Scalene Triangle	A triangle in which there are no congruent sides or angles	
Hypotenuse	The diagonal line opposite the right angle in a right triangle	Hypotenuse

Common Mathematics/Geometry Symbols and Terms (cont.)

Term	Symbol/Definition	Example
Legs	The other two sides of a right triangle, adjacent to the hypotenuse and forming the right angle	Legs → h
Pythagorean Theorem	The square of the hypotenuse of a right triangle is equal to the sum of the squares of the legs	Let h represent the hypotenuse, s_1 represent one leg or side and s_2 represent the other leg or side. $h^2 = s_1{}^2 + s_2{}^2$ $h^2 = 3^2 + 2^2$ $h^2 = 13$ $h = \sqrt{13}$ 3 in. (s_1), h, 2 in. (s_2)
Similar Triangles	Triangles that have congruent angles and corresponding sides that are proportional in length	
Congruent Triangles	Triangles that have corresponding sides and angles equal	
Median	A segment whose endpoints are a vertex of the triangle and the midpoint of the opposite side	Median
Altitude	A segment from a vertex that is perpendicular to the opposite side or to the line that is an extension of the opposite	Altitude
Perpendicular Bisector	A line segment, a ray, or a plane that is perpendicular to a given segment and bisects it	

Chapter 1: Introduction to Geometry

Introduction to the Concepts of Geometry

Geometry is a branch of mathematics that studies the sizes and shapes of objects. The word geometry means *earth* (geo) *measure* (metry). The study of geometry explores shapes, their properties, and relationships. Geometry is also the study of patterns, finding similarities, and optical illusions. Skills learned in algebra will help with your study of geometry. In geometry you will be solving equations, making graphs, and problem solving like you did in algebra. The first section of this worktext will introduce you to the concepts of geometry.

Concepts of Geometry

① Shapes

② Congruence and Similarity

③ Symmetry

    Ⓐ Line or Reflection Symmetry

    Ⓑ Rotation

    Ⓒ Translation

    Ⓓ Glide Reflection

Explanations of the Concepts of Geometry

① **Shapes**

Studying the characteristics or attributes of objects is an important part of studying geometry. In how many ways can the objects below be grouped?

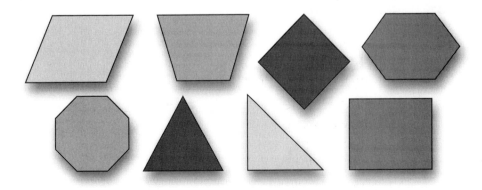

These objects could be grouped by number of sides or by shape.

Chapter 1: Introduction to Geometry

Polygons have names determined by the number of sides: triangles have three sides, quadrilaterals have four sides, pentagons have five sides, hexagons have six sides, and octagons have eight sides.

The polygons on the previous page are in one plane, or surface. Objects can also be solid, three-dimensional, and in more than one plane. Notice the differences among the objects below and the ones on the previous page. The objects below have depth as well as length and width.

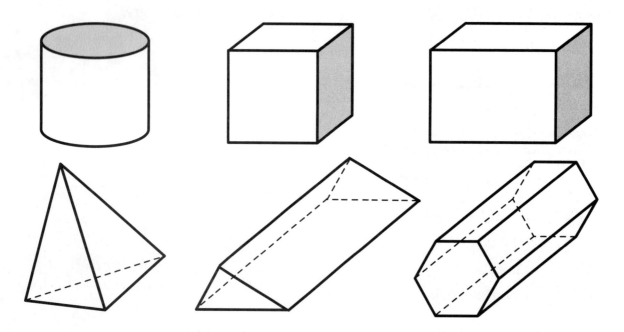

❷   Congruence and Similarity

Two figures are **congruent** if they have the same shape and the same size. Figures can be congruent without having the same orientation.

Examples of congruent objects:

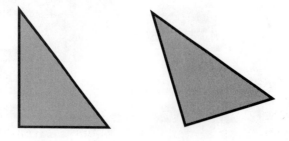

Chapter 1: Introduction to Geometry (cont.)

Examples of objects that are not congruent:

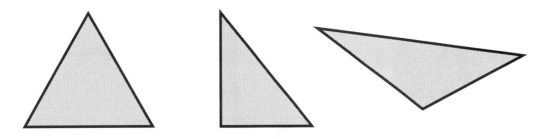

Geometric figures are **similar** if the figures have the same shape. They may or may not have the same size.

Examples of similar figures:

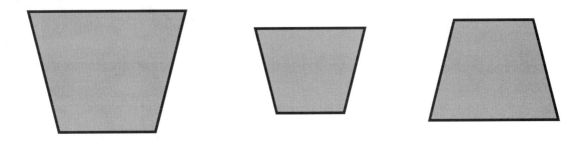

Examples of figures that are not similar:

❸ Symmetry

Ⓐ Line or Reflection Symmetry

If a figure can be divided into two parts, each of which is a mirror image of the other, it has **line symmetry**, or **reflection symmetry**. Symmetry is found in nature. A picture of an animal's face demonstrates line symmetry, and a spider's body shows line symmetry.

Chapter 1: Introduction to Geometry (cont.)

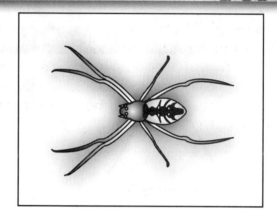

Symmetry can also be found in non-living things. The pictures below show line symmetry. The windmill structure shows line symmetry, and the blades show both line and rotational symmetry. The white chess piece shows line symmetry down the center.

A figure in a plane has a line of symmetry if it can be mapped onto itself by a reflection. The star below has vertical symmetry because a vertical line can be drawn, and the star can be folded in so all of the points overlap, or a mirror can be put on the line, and it will reflect the rest of the star. The star also has four other lines of symmetry. The circle below has vertical and horizontal symmetry as well as other lines of symmetry because it can be folded or reflected on itself from the vertical line or the horizontal line. The smiley face has vertical symmetry.

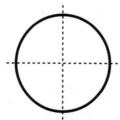

Chapter 1: Introduction to Geometry (cont.)

B Rotation

A figure has 180° rotational symmetry if the figure can be mapped onto itself by a rotation of 180°. For example, the diamond shown below has rotational symmetry. If you rotate it 180° clockwise around its center, the resulting figure coincides with the original figure. Note that there can be other rotational numbers. For example, an equilateral triangle has 120° rotational symmetry, and a square has 90° rotational symmetry.

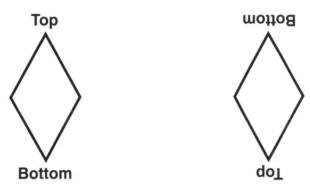

C Translation

Translational symmetry is created when an object is moved without rotating or reflecting it.

D Glide Reflection

Glide reflection symmetry is a transformation that consists of a translation by a vector followed by a reflection in a line that is parallel to the vector.

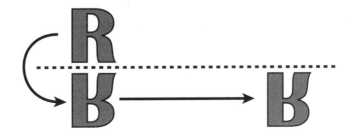

Date: _____

Chapter 1: Introduction to Geometry (cont.)

Practice Problems for Geometry

1. **Directions:** Sort these objects into groups based on shape. Connect the objects that are in the same category with a line.

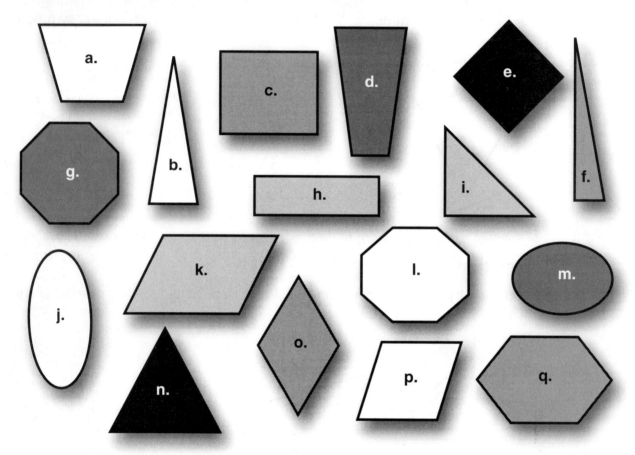

Explain how you grouped these objects. What were the different categories of shapes?

_____

_____

_____

_____

2. Which of these figures are congruent?

A. 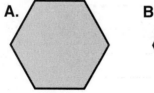   B.   C.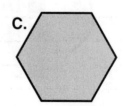

Name: _____ Date: _____

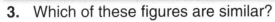

Chapter 1: Introduction to Geometry (cont.)

3. Which of these figures are similar?

A. 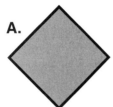   B. 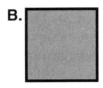   C.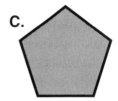

Directions: In questions 4–6, divide the shaded region into two congruent parts.

4. 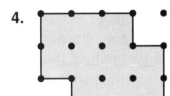   **5.** 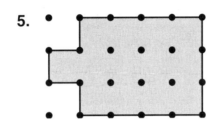   **6.**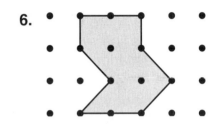

7. Starting with a square piece of paper, try to divide the paper into four squares, six squares, seven squares, eight squares, nine squares, and ten squares. Not all of the squares need to be congruent.

8. Which figures have 180° rotational symmetry?

A.    B. 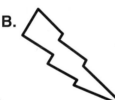   C. 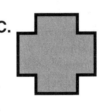   D. 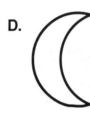   E.

9. Which figure has horizontal symmetry? Which has vertical symmetry?

A. _____    B. _____

10. Does this object have symmetry? Explain.

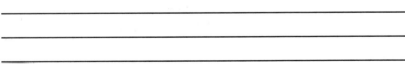

_____

_____

_____

_____

_____

Chapter 1: Introduction to Geometry (cont.)

Summary of Introduction to Geometry

The study of geometry explores shapes, their properties, and relationships. Studying the characteristics or attributes of objects is an important part of studying geometry.

Polygons have names determined by the number of sides: triangles have three sides, quadrilaterals have four sides, pentagons have five sides, hexagons have six sides, and octagons have eight sides.

Two figures are congruent if they have the same shape and the same size. Figures can be congruent without having the same orientation. Geometric figures are similar if the figures have the same shape. They may or may not be the same size.

If a figure can be divided into two parts, each of which is a mirror image of the other, then it has line symmetry, or reflection symmetry. A figure in a plane has a line of symmetry if it can be mapped onto itself by a reflection. A figure has 180° rotational symmetry if the figure can be mapped onto itself by a rotation of 180°. Figures can also have rotational symmetry of 120°, 90°, etc. Translational symmetry is created when an object is moved without rotating or reflecting it. Glide reflection symmetry is a transformation that consists of a translation by a vector followed by a reflection in a line that is parallel to the vector.

Tips to Remember for Geometry

The study of geometry is often about motion, change, and similarity. When working with geometry, think about the following questions.

- How are these objects the same? How are these objects different?
- How can I change the object's position with symmetry moves from one location to another?
- How can I partition the geometric figure into different shapes?
- What relationship will I need to see to understand more about the shape?

Real Life Applications of Geometry

Scientists use classification systems to group different kinds of animals. The groups are created by the plant or animal's characteristics or attributes. The classification of living things is based on these groups: kingdom, phylum, class, order, genus, and species.

Factories use congruent objects when they are mass-producing parts for cars and other machinery, and the parts must be exactly the same for each machine.

Chapter 1: Introduction to Geometry (cont.)

Geometry is used to study patterns in chromosome structure and in living and non-living things. It is also used in interior design and making scale objects. Engineers use geometry to design and construct support structures in buildings and highways. Pilots of boats, planes, and spaceships use geometry to navigate. Armed forces need to know geometry to navigate and to fire missiles and guns. Geometry is used in putting in shelves, to figure out how much gravel is needed for a road, or for making patterns for clothes.

Symmetry is found in nature and many objects that are in the world. Symmetry in our natural world is found in snowflakes, flowers, and animals. Symmetry in non-living things can be found in sink drains, car wheels, quilt patterns, capital letters of the alphabet, inkblots, rugs, religious symbols, and wallpaper.

Chapter 2: Coordinate and Non-Coordinate Geometry

Introduction to Coordinate and Non-Coordinate Geometry

A **coordinate** is a point on a line that can be matched one-to-one with real numbers. The number that is matched with the point is called a coordinate. In a plane, the points can be matched one-to-one with ordered pairs of real numbers (x, y). The x is called the x-coordinate, and the y is called the y-coordinate. On a graph, the y-axis is the vertical axis, and the x-axis is the horizontal axis. In Algebra I there was a discussion of two coordinate systems: real number lines and coordinate planes. On the **number line**, the points have a single number. A **coordinate plane** is a two-dimensional system in which each point has two coordinates.

Number Line   A = -3   B = 2

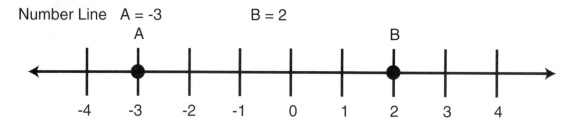

Coordinate Plane M = (7, 4)   D = (1, -2)   A = (-2, 7)

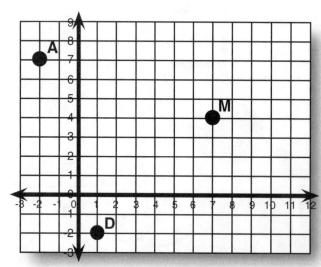

Concepts of Coordinate and Non-Coordinate Geometry

1 Midpoint Formula

2 Slope

3 Equations

4 Distance of Line Segments

Chapter 2: Coordinate and Non-Coordinate Geometry (cont.)

Explanations of Concepts of Coordinate and Non-Coordinate Geometry

❶ Midpoint Formula

The **midpoint** of a line segment is the single point that is an equal distance from both ends. In coordinate geometry, you can use the following formula to determine the midpoint of a segment. Let $A (x_1, y_1)$ and $B (x_2, y_2)$ be points in a coordinate plane. The midpoint of $\overline{AB}$ is $\left(\dfrac{x_1 + x_2}{2}, \dfrac{y_1 + y_2}{2}\right)$. This is called the midpoint formula. To find the midpoint of a line segment, find the endpoints; add the two x-coordinates and divide by 2; and add the two y-coordinates and divide by 2. That is, the x- and y-coordinates of the midpoint are the average of the x- and y-coordinates respective of the endpoints. The two points you get are the coordinates of the midpoint of the line.

Example of finding the midpoint of a segment:

Problem: Find the midpoint if
$M = (7, 4)$ $D = (1, -2)$

Step 1:   Let $M = (x_1, y_1)$ and $D = (x_2, y_2)$.

The midpoint of $\overline{DM} = \left(\dfrac{x_1 + x_2}{2}, \dfrac{y_1 + y_2}{2}\right)$

Step 2:   Substitute the coordinates for
M and D and solve.

$\left(\dfrac{7 + 1}{2}, \dfrac{4 + -2}{2}\right)$

$\left(\dfrac{8}{2}, \dfrac{2}{2}\right) = (4, 1)$

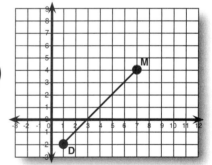

Answer: The midpoint of $\overline{DM}$ is at (4, 1).

Chapter 2: Coordinate and Non-Coordinate Geometry (cont.)

② Slope

In the coordinate plane, the slope is used to describe the steepness of a line. The slope is the measure of the incline of the line. If the slope is positive, the line goes up when moving from left to right; if the slope is negative, the line goes down when moving from left to right. The letter m is often used to represent the slope of a line.

Properties of slope include the following:

A. The slope, m, of a line that contains (x_1, y_1) and (x_2, y_2), is:

$$\text{slope} = m = \frac{rise}{run} = \frac{y_2 - y_1}{x_2 - x_1}$$

B. Two lines are parallel if and only if they have the same slope, $m_1 = m_2$.

C. Two lines with slopes of m_1 and m_2 are perpendicular if and only if m_2 is the negative reciprocal of m_1. That is, $m_2 = -\frac{1}{m_1}$. This also means that $m_1 \cdot m_2 = -1$.

Example of finding the slope of a line:

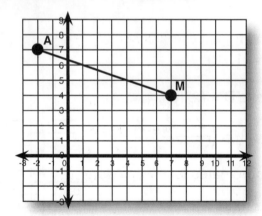

Problem: The line on the graph above contains M = (7, 4) and A = (-2, 7). Find the slope of the line.

A. The formula for slope: $m = \frac{rise}{run} = \frac{y_2 - y_1}{x_2 - x_1}$

Step 1: Substitute the values of x and y.

$$m = \frac{rise}{run} = \frac{7 - 4}{-2 - 7}$$

Step 2: Solve: $\frac{7 - 4}{-2 - 7} = \frac{3}{-9} = -\frac{1}{3}$

Answer: The slope of the line is $-\frac{1}{3}$.

Chapter 2: Coordinate and Non-Coordinate Geometry (cont.)

Example of identifying parallel lines:

B. Two lines are parallel if and only if they have the same slope.

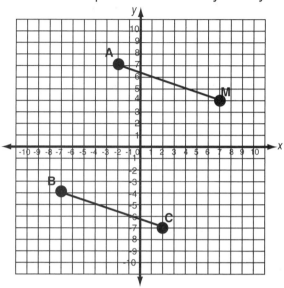

The line on the graph above contains the points $M = (7, 4)$ and $A = (-2, 7)$. We found the slope of that line to be $-\frac{1}{3}$.

Problem: If $B = (-7, -4)$ and $C = (2, -7)$, find the slope.

The formula for slope: $m = \dfrac{rise}{run} = \dfrac{y_2 - y_1}{x_2 - x_1}$

Step 1: Substitute the coordinates for the points on $\overline{BC}$.

$m = \dfrac{rise}{run} = \dfrac{-7 - -4}{2 - -7}$

Step 2: Solve: $m = \dfrac{-7 - -4}{2 - -7} = \dfrac{-3}{9} = -\dfrac{1}{3}$

Answer: So, two lines with the same slope are parallel.

Example of identifying perpendicular lines:

C. Two lines with slopes of m_1 and m_2 are perpendicular if and only if m_2 is the negative reciprocal of m_1. This means that $m_1 \bullet m_2 = -1$.

Chapter 2: Coordinate and Non-Coordinate Geometry (cont.)

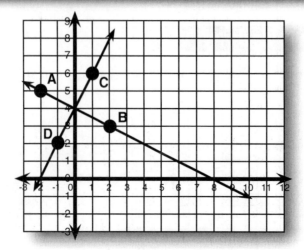

Problem:	Consider $\overline{AB}$, where $A = (-2, 5)$ and $B = (2, 3)$.	Consider $\overline{DC}$, where $D = (-1, 2)$ and $C = (1, 6)$:
	$m = \dfrac{rise}{run} = \dfrac{y_2 - y_1}{x_2 - x_1}$	$m = \dfrac{rise}{run} = \dfrac{y_2 - y_1}{x_2 - x_1}$
Step 1:	$m = \dfrac{3 - 5}{2 - \text{-}2} = \dfrac{-2}{4} = -\dfrac{1}{2}$	$m = \dfrac{6 - 2}{1 - \text{-}1} = \dfrac{4}{2} = 2$
Answer:	The slope of $\overline{AB}$ is $\dfrac{1}{2}$.	The slope of $\overline{DC}$ is 2.

The two lines are perpendicular if $m_1 \bullet m_2 = -1$, so the lines are perpendicular.

The study of geometry with a focus on **coordinate geometry** is also called **analytical geometry**. Coordinate geometry uses coordinate systems to study segments, lines, planes, and other figures. **Euclidean geometry**, or **non-coordinate geometry**, does not use coordinate systems. That means that you do not have to use grids to study the relationships of points and lines. Line q seems to be perpendicular to p, and m and q seem to be parallel.

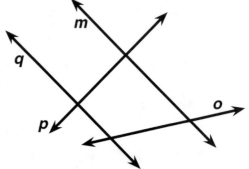

❸   Equations

Equations can be changed to the slope-intercept form by solving the equation for y. In this case, the form $y = mx + b$ is used where m is the slope of the line, and b tells where the equation intercepts the y-axis.

Chapter 2: Coordinate and Non-Coordinate Geometry (cont.)

Example of the slope-intercept method:

Problem: Given the equation $2x + y - 2 = 0$, solve for y.

Step 1: $2x + y - 2 - 2x = 0 - 2x$

$y - 2 = -2x$

$y - 2 + 2 = -2x + 2$

$y = -2x + 2$

Answer: The slope of this line $= -2$.

The y-intercept is 2, and the line intercepts the y-axis at point (0, 2).

The slope-intercept form can be graphed on a coordinate plane. To graph using the slope-intercept method: express the equation in terms of a single y, so it has the form of $y = mx + b$. Remember that b is the y-intercept or where the line crosses the y-axis, so mark the number for the b term on the y-axis. If there is no term for b, then the intercept is 0. The number in front of the x (represented in this form by m) is the slope. To graph the line, the slope must be written as a fraction. If it is already a fraction, then leave it. If it is an integer, put the integer over 1: $\left(\frac{m}{1}\right)$. Start at the y-intercept, and move along the x-axis the number of spaces in the denominator. If the fraction is positive, move up the number of spaces in the numerator. If it is negative, move down the number of spaces in the numerator. Mark this point. Draw a line to connect both points.

Example of graphing using the intercept method:

Problem: $2y - 4x = 8$

Step 1: Put the equation into the y form:

$2y - 4x + 4x = 8 + 4x$

$2y = 4x + 8$

$\dfrac{2y}{2} = \dfrac{4x + 8}{2}$

$y = 2x + 4$

Chapter 2: Coordinate and Non-Coordinate Geometry (cont.)

Step 2: Using the form $y = mx + b$, 4 is the y-intercept, and 2 is the slope. It is an integer, so think of it as $\frac{2}{1}$. The denominator is 1, so move right 1 space.

Step 3: The numerator is 2, and the fraction is positive, so move up 2 spaces to the point (1, 6).

Step 4: Draw a line connecting the two points.

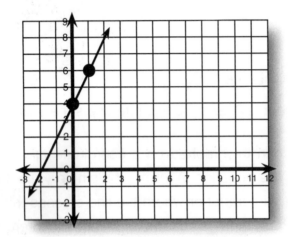

Step 5: Check the answer by substituting the point (1, 6) in the equation.

$2y - 4x = 8$

$2(6) - 4(1) =$

$12 - 4 = 8$

$8 = 8$

The solution is correct.

The equation of a line can be found if you know the slope and a point on the line. Use the form for finding the intercept $y = mx + b$. Substitute the slope and the coordinates for the point and solve for b. Then substitute m and b into the equation $y = mx + b$.

Chapter 2: Coordinate and Non-Coordinate Geometry (cont.)

Example of finding the equation of a line using slope-intercept:

Problem: The slope is -5, and one point is (-2,-1).

Use the form $y = mx + b$.

Step 1:   Substitute the slope and the point.

$-1 = -5(-2) + b$

$-1 = 10 + b$

$-1 - 10 = 10 + b - 10$

$-11 = b$

Step 2:   Substitute m and b in the equation to get the equation of the line.

$y = -5x - 11$

The equation for a line can also be found using the **two-point method**. Using this method, find the slope of the line by finding the change in x and the change in y. Find the change by subtracting one pair of coordinates from the other. Find the slope by dividing the change in y by the change in x. Substitute the slope into the form $y = mx + b$. Substitute one pair of coordinates into the equation and solve for b. Substitute the slope and b into the equation to find the equation of the line.

Example of finding the equation of a line using two points:

Problem: Points (3, 4) and (6, 2)

Step 1:   Find the change by subtracting one pair of coordinates from the other.

Change in $y = 4 - 2 = 2$

Change in $x = 3 - 6 = -3$

Step 2:   Divide the change in y by the change in $x = -\frac{2}{3}$.

$-\frac{2}{3}$ is the slope.

Chapter 2: Coordinate and Non-Coordinate Geometry (cont.)

Step 3: Substitute the slope and one pair of coordinates and solve for *b*.

$y = mx + b$

$4 = -\frac{2}{3}(3) + b$

$4 = -2 + b$

$4 + 2 = -2 + b + 2$

$b = 6$

Answer: So the equation for the line is $y = -\frac{2}{3}x + 6$ or $3y = -2x + 18$.

4 Length of Line Segments

The length of a line segment is the distance between the two endpoints of the segment. Distance is measured in linear measurements such as meters, centimeters, inches, feet, etc. To find the distance, find the endpoints, subtract the smaller *x*-coordinate from the larger *x*-coordinate and square the difference; subtract the smaller *y*-coordinate from the larger *y*-coordinate and square the difference; add the two squared differences and find the square root. The square root is the distance from one endpoint to the other. The formula for finding the distance between any two points (x_1, y_1) and (x_2, y_2) is $\sqrt{(x_2 - x_1)^2 + (y_2 - y_1)^2}$.

Example of finding the distance:

Problem: Find the distance between (5, 5) and (1, 2).

Step 1: $\sqrt{(5-1)^2 + (5-2)^2}$

Step 2: $\sqrt{(4)^2 + (3)^2}$

Step 3: $\sqrt{16 + 9}$

Step 4: $\sqrt{25} = 5$

Answer: So the distance between the two points is 5 units.

Name: _____ Date: _____

Chapter 2: Coordinate and Non-Coordinate Geometry (cont.)

Practice: Coordinate and Non-Coordinate Geometry

Show your work for these practice problems on your own paper.

Finding the Midpoint

Directions: Find the midpoints of the lines in problems 1–4 using the given endpoints. Check by graphing the results on your own paper.

1. (6, 4) and (-2, 6) _____

2. (-3, -3) and (5, 5) _____

3. (3, -2) and (5, 12) _____

4. (2, 8) and (2, 3) _____

Finding Slope

Directions: Use the formula for slope to solve problems 5–7. Use a coordinate plane to help solve these problems.

5. Find the slope between (3, 0) and (0, -2).

6. Find the slope between (-5, 1) and (5,-1).

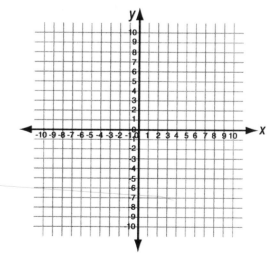

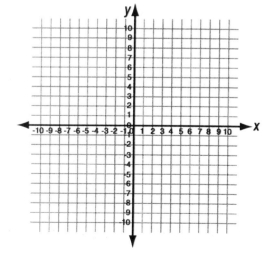

Date: _____

2: Coordinate and Non-Coordinate Geometry (cont.)

7. Find the slope between (0, 0) and (5, 3).

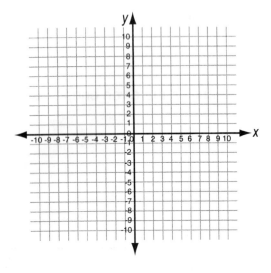

Directions: For questions 8–10, find the slope of each of the pairs of lines. Draw the lines on the coordinate plane. Explain which are parallel and which are perpendicular.

8. $\overleftrightarrow{AB}$ goes through A (-2, 1) and B (1, 2);
$\overleftrightarrow{CD}$ goes through C (-1, 3) and D (0, 0).

9. $\overleftrightarrow{EF}$ goes through E (-2, 1) and F (1, 2);
$\overleftrightarrow{GH}$ goes through G (2, 1) and H (5, 2).

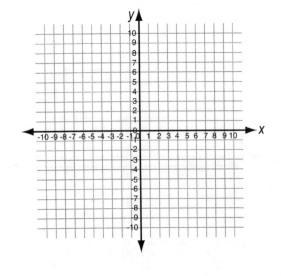

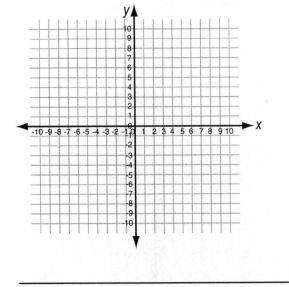

_____   _____

_____   _____

_____   _____

Name: _____ Date: _____

Chapter 2: Coordinate and Non-Coordinate Geometry (cont.)

10. $\overleftrightarrow{IJ}$ goes through I (-2, 1) and J (1, 2);
$\overleftrightarrow{KL}$ goes through K (-1, 2) and L (2, 3).

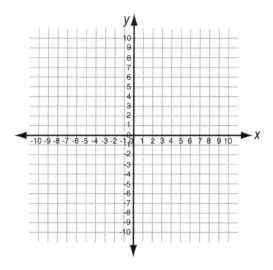

_____

_____

_____

Equations

Directions: Using the slope-intercept formula, find the slope and graph the line.

11. $5x - y + 2 = 0$ **12.** $4x + 2y = -8$

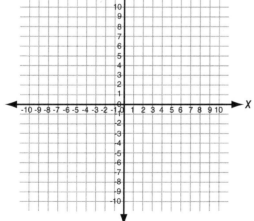   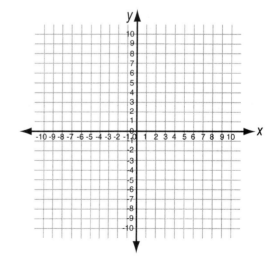

Name: _____   Date: _____

Chapter 2: Coordinate and Non-Coordinate Geometry (cont.)

13. $y + 3 - 3x = 0$

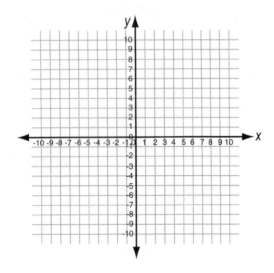

Directions: Find the equation of the line using the intercept method.

14. Slope = 2, Point (4, -4) _____

15. Slope = $\frac{1}{2}$, Point (0, -1) _____

Directions: Find the equation of the line using the two-point method.

16. (1, 1) and (6, 2) _____

17. (0, 5) and (2, 0) _____

18. (3, -1) and (4, -2) _____

Directions: Find the distance between two points.

19. (4, 2) and (1, 6) _____

20. (-3, 2) and (4, -1) _____

Chapter 2: Coordinate and Non-Coordinate Geometry (cont.)

Summary of Coordinate and Non-Coordinate Geometry

Coordinate geometry is also called analytical geometry. Coordinate geometry uses coordinate systems to study segments, lines, planes, and other figures. The midpoint of a line segment is the single point that is an equal distance from both ends. In coordinate geometry, you can use the following formula to determine the midpoint of a segment. Let A (x_1, y_1) and B (x_2, y_2) be points in a coordinate plane. The midpoint of $\overline{AB}$ is $\left(\dfrac{x_1 + x_2}{2}, \dfrac{y_1 + y_2}{2}\right)$.

In the coordinate plane, the slope is used to describe the steepness of a line. The slope is the measure of the incline of the line.

Properties of slope include the following:

A. The slope, m, of a line that contains (x_1, y_1) and (x_2, y_2), is:

$$\text{slope} = m = \frac{rise}{run} = \frac{y_2 - y_1}{x_2 - x_1}$$

B. Two lines are parallel if and only if they have the same slope.

C. Two lines with slopes of m_1 and m_2 are perpendicular if and only if m_2 is the negative reciprocal of m_1. That is, $m_2 = -\dfrac{1}{m_1}$. This also means that $m_1 \cdot m_2 = -1$.

Equations for a line can be changed to the slope-intercept form by solving the equation for y and using the form $y = mx + b$. In this form, m is the slope, and b is the y-intercept of the line. The equation of a line can be found if you know the slope and a point on the line and use the formula to find the intercept: $y = mx + b$. The equation for a line can also be found using the two-point method.

The length of a line segment is the distance between the two endpoints of the segment. The formula for finding the distance between any two points (x_1, y_1) and (x_2, y_2) is $\sqrt{(x_2 - x_1)^2 + (y_2 - y_1)^2}$.

Tips to Remember for Coordinate and Non-Coordinate Geometry

If the slope is positive, the line increases (goes up) when moving from left to right. If it is negative, it decreases (goes down) when moving from left to right.

The larger the absolute value of the slope of the line, the steeper the line is.

Lines can be seen as parallel by changing each equation to slope-intercept form and finding out if the slopes are equal. Similarly, if the two slopes represented by m_1 and m_2 are multiplied ($m_1 \cdot m_2$) and the product is -1, then the lines are perpendicular.

Chapter 2: Coordinate and Non-Coordinate Geometry (cont.)

Real Life Applications of Coordinate and Non-Coordinate Geometry

Because business situations can be expressed as a linear relationship, the idea of slope can be used in business situations. For example, the relationship of $0.04x + 45$ expresses the charges of a phone service where a person pays $45 a month plus $0.04 per minute of long-distance. Slope can also be used to determine sales trends in business.

Chapter 3: Angles

Introduction to the Concepts of Angles

The discussion of angles begins with a look at rays. A **ray** consists of an initial point and all of the points going in the same direction away from the initial point. For example, using *A* as the initial point, all of the points going to the right of *A* will be on the ray going toward *B*. This ray can be represented by $\overrightarrow{AB}$.

The ray below could be represented by $\overleftarrow{BA}$.

An **angle** is two rays with the same endpoint. The rays are the sides of the angle. In the figure below, we have two rays $\overrightarrow{AB}$ and $\overrightarrow{AC}$. Both of these rays are connected at the same point, with point *A* forming the angle with points BAC.

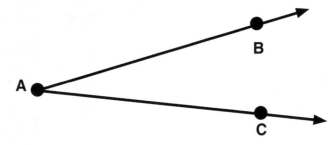

Concepts of Angles

1 Introduction to Angles

    A Measuring Angles

    B Classifying Angles

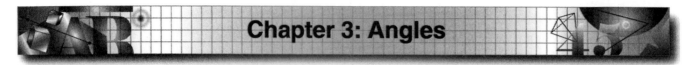

Explanations of the Concepts of Angles

❶ Introduction to Angles

As stated above, an **angle** is two rays with the same endpoint. The rays are the sides of the angle. In the figure below, we have two rays $\vec{AB}$ and $\vec{AC}$. Both of these rays are connected at the same point, point A forming the angle with points BAC. The common endpoint A is called the **vertex**. A vertex is the common point where the two rays are connected. The sides of the angle are the rays $\vec{AB}$ and $\vec{AC}$. The angle could be labeled angle *BAC* or *CAB*. Note that because A is the vertex, it must go in the middle of the three letters representing the angle. This can also be written as $\angle BAC$ or $\angle CAB$.

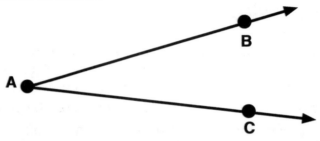

An angle can also be labeled using the letter at the vertex, so the angle could also be labeled $\angle A$.

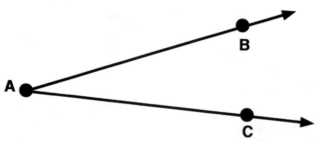

An angle can also be labeled using a number inside its vertex. When using a number to label the angle, make a small arc inside the angle, so the angle could just be labeled $\angle 1$.

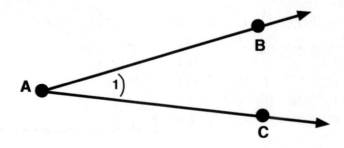

Chapter 3: Angles (cont.)

An angle divides a plane into three different areas. Points *X*, *Y*, and *Z* show where these areas are. *X* represents a point exterior of ∠BAC. *Y* represents a point interior of the angle. *Z* represents a point on the angle itself. Note that *A*, *B*, and *C* are also points on the angle.

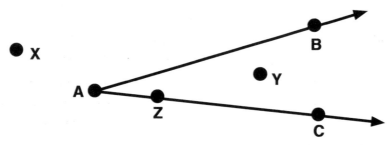

Ⓐ Measuring Angles

Lines and line segments can be measured with a ruler. Angles can be measured using a protractor. A **protractor** is an instrument used to construct and measure angles. Angles can be measured in degrees. The semi-circular degree protractor is marked off into 180 parts, or **degrees**. When an angle like ∠CDF is measured, the measure can be written as "the measure of the angle CDF is 90 degrees" or m∠CDF = 90°.

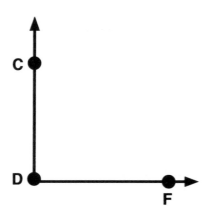

Examine the protractor at the right. Note that there are numbers from 0 to 180. Each of these numbers represents the number of degrees. There are 360° around a circle; 180° is the distance halfway around the circle. The numbers are marked from left to right and right to left around the semi-circle. There is also a mark at the center of the straight edge of the protractor.

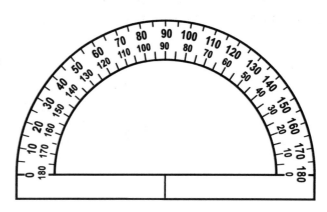

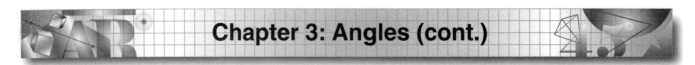

Chapter 3: Angles (cont.)

To measure an angle using a protractor, place the center mark on the straight edge of the protractor over the vertex of the angle. Place the horizontal line of the protractor along one side of the angle. Read the number where the other ray crosses or intersects the protractor. This is the measure of the angle.

Example of measuring angles using a protractor:

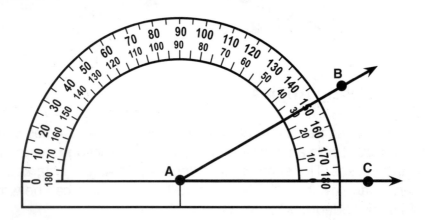

The intersection of $\overrightarrow{AB}$ with the protractor above is 30°, so the measure of the angle BAC is 30 degrees, or m∠BAC = 30°.

Example of measuring angles using a protractor:

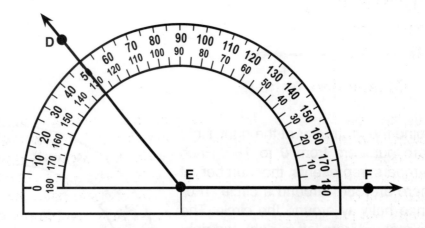

The intersection of $\overrightarrow{ED}$ with the protractor above is 130°, so the measure of the angle DEF is 130 degrees or m∠DEF = 130°.

Sometimes the angles may be greater than 180°. Angles that are greater than 180° are shown by adding a small arc to the angle. To measure ∠FGH, measure the small angle, and then subtract the small angle from 360°.

Chapter 3: Angles (cont.)

Example of using a protractor to measure an angle greater than 180°:

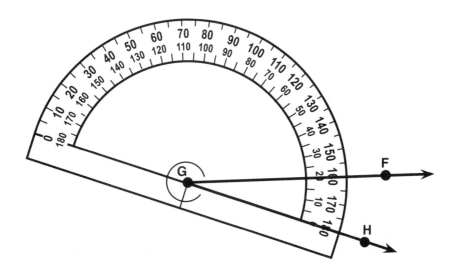

This angle has an arc indicating that the angle is greater than 180°. The measure of the small angle is 20°. Subtract the small angle from 360°.

m∠FGH = 360° − 20°

The difference is 340°.

m∠FGH = 340°

B Classifying Angles

Angles can be classified into different groups. These groups include acute, right, obtuse, straight, and reflex. **Acute angles** are less than 90°. **Right angles** measure exactly 90°. **Obtuse angles** are more than 90°, but less than 180°. **Straight angles** are exactly 180°. **Reflex angles** are greater than 180°, but less than 360°. Two angles can be considered vertical, complementary, supplementary, congruent, adjacent, or linear pairs. Two angles are **vertical** if their rays form two pairs of opposite rays. Two angles are **complementary** if the two angles add up to 90°. Two angles are **supplementary** if the two angles add up to 180° and form a straight line. Two angles are **congruent** if they have the same measure. **Adjacent angles** share a common vertex and side but have no common interior points. An **angle bisector** is a ray that divides an angle into two equal parts. Two adjacent angles form a **linear pair** if their non-common sides are opposite rays.

 **Chapter 3: Angles (cont.)**

Examples of acute angles:

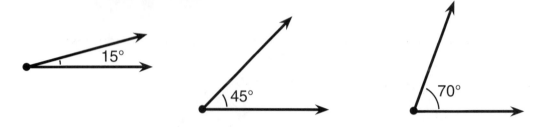

These angles are all less than 90°, so they are acute angles.

Examples of right angles:

These angles are right angles because they are both 90° angles.

Examples of obtuse angles:

These angles are both obtuse because they are more than 90°, but less than 180°.

Chapter 3: Angles (cont.)

Example of a straight angle:

180°

This is a straight angle because it is exactly 180°.

Examples of reflex angles:

280°

325°

These are reflex angles because they are greater than 180° but less than 360°.

Examples of vertical angles:

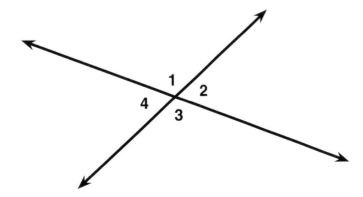

1   2
4   3

Angles 1 and 3 are vertical angles because their sides form two pairs of opposite rays. Angles 2 and 4 are vertical angles because their sides also form two pairs of opposite rays.

Chapter 3: Angles (cont.)

Example of complementary angles:

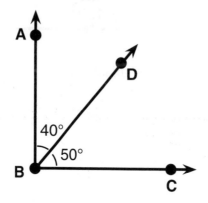

∠ABD is 40°, and ∠DBC is 50°. ∠ABD and ∠DBC are complementary angles because their sum is equal to 90°.

Example of supplementary angles:

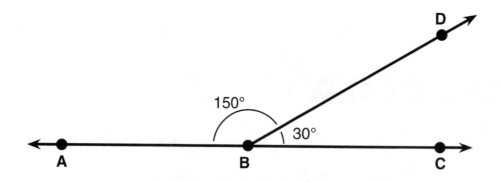

∠ABD and ∠DBC are supplementary because together the measures of the angles add up to 180° or a straight line.

Examples of congruent angles:

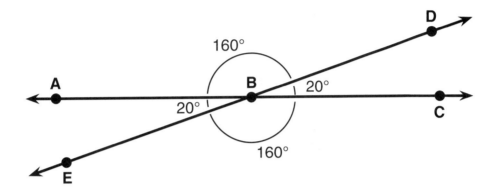

∠ABD and ∠EBC both have the same measure, so they are congruent. ∠ABE and ∠DBC both have the same measure, so they are also congruent.

Example of an angle bisector:

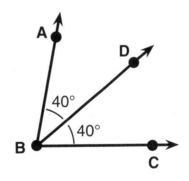

The angle bisector is $\overrightarrow{BD}$ because it divides ∠ABC into two equal parts.

Chapter 3: Angles (cont.)

Example of adjacent angles:

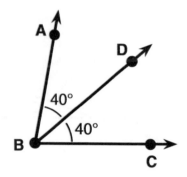

∠ABD is adjacent to ∠DBC because they share a common side and do not have any common interior points.

Examples of linear pairs:

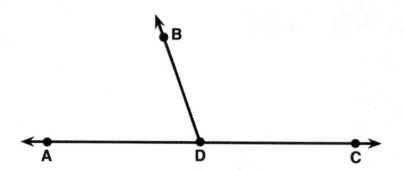

∠ADB and ∠BDC are linear pairs because they are adjacent angles, and the non-common sides are opposite rays.

Name: _____ Date: _____

Chapter 3: Angles (cont.)

Practice: Angles

Directions: Using a protractor, measure the angles.

1. m ∠ = _____

2. m ∠ = _____

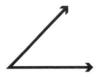

3. m ∠ = _____

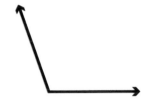

4. m ∠ = _____

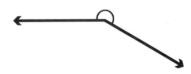

5. m ∠ = _____

Directions: Use the words in the Word Bank to complete the blanks for questions 6–15. Then draw an appropriate angle below each question.

Word Bank

acute	adjacent	complementary	congruent
linear pair	obtuse	reflex	right
straight	supplementary	vertical	

ame: _____ Date: _____

Chapter 3: Angles (cont.)

6. _____ angles are two angles that are exactly the same size and shape and have the same measure.

Draw an example.

7. _____ angles are greater than 180°, but less than 360°.

Draw an example.

8. _____ angles measure exactly 180°.

Draw an example.

9. _____ angles are more than 90°, but less than 180°.

Draw an example.

10. _____ angles are less than 90°.

Draw an example.

Name: _____ Date: _____

 **Chapter 3: Angles (cont.)**

11. _____ angles are two angles that have a total measure of 90°.

Draw an example.

12. _____ angles are two angles that have a total measure of 180°.

Draw an example.

13. _____ angles are formed when two lines intersect. These opposite angles always have the same measure.

Draw an example.

14. Two _____ angles share a common side and a common vertex but do not share any interior points.

Draw an example.

15. An angle _____ is a ray that divides an angle into two equal parts.

Draw an example.

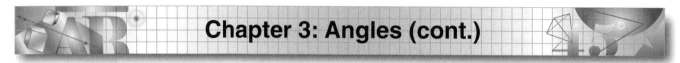

Chapter 3: Angles (cont.)

Summary of Angles

An angle is two rays with the same endpoint. Angles can be measured using a protractor. Angles can be classified into different groups. These groups include acute, right, obtuse, straight, and reflex. Two angles can be considered vertical, complementary, supplementary, congruent, adjacent, or linear pairs. An angle bisector is a ray that divides an angle into equal parts.

Tips to Remember for Angles

- When using a protractor to measure angles over 180°, measure the smaller angle and subtract the measure from 360°.
- Always pay attention to the way an angle is labeled. Learn the differences between acute, obtuse, straight, right, and reflex angles.

Real Life Applications of Angles

Angles can be used to measure rocket trajectory. They can also be used to measure the heights of objects such as trees and tall buildings that are too large to measure with a ruler. When building roads, engineers must consider the angle of the incline or decline of the road. Many racetracks have inclines or "banks" in the turns so drivers can maintain high speeds without going off the track.

Chapter 4: Patterns and Reasoning

Introduction to the Concepts of Patterns and Reasoning

Reasoning in geometry usually consists of three parts. One part is using inductive reasoning to look for patterns. **Inductive reasoning** is making a conjecture about several examples after looking for a pattern. The second part is **making conjectures**. Making conjectures means making inferences based on inclusive evidence. The third part of reasoning in geometry is **verifying the conjectures** made using logical reasoning. This section will examine these three parts of geometry.

Concepts of Patterns and Reasoning

1 Exploring Patterns

2 The Structure of Geometry

3 Angle Addition Postulate

4 Conditional Statements

5 Deductive Reasoning

Explanations of the Concepts of Patterns and Reasoning

1 **Exploring Patterns**

Looking for patterns is the first stage of geometry. A pattern can be an artistic design, a model to be followed, a composite of traits, an ideal worthy of imitation, or a representative sample. A pattern can also mean to make, model, form, or design by following a pattern. A **pattern** has three characteristics: a unit, repetition, and a system of organization. Patterns can be found in numbers, nature, art, and construction.

Examples of patterns:

Fibonacci Numbers {0, 1, 1, 2, 3, 5, 8, 13, …}. In this pattern, you add the last two digits to get the next. That is, 0 + 1 = 1, 1 + 1 = 2, 1 + 2 = 3, 2 + 3 = 5, etc.

Counting is based on patterns of the decimal number system that is based on 10 digits: {0, 1, 2, 3, 4, 5, 6, 7, 8, 9}.

Pascal's Triangle: Although Blaise Pascal was not the first to study the arithmetical triangle now known as Pascal's Triangle, he did make more contributions to it than anyone else ever did, around the year 1653.

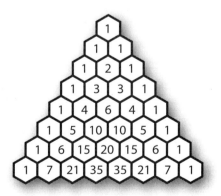

Pascal's Triangle

The triangle is constructed in such a way that each number is the sum of the numbers above it and to the left of it. See illustration at above right.

Chapter 4: Patterns and Reasoning (cont.)

Binary Codes Used in Computers

Binary Number	2^4	2^3	2^2	2^1	2^0	Decimal Equivalent
10				1	0	2
111			1	1	1	7
10101	1	0	1	0	1	21
11110	1	1	1	1	0	30

A honeycomb is made of hexagonal combs.

Patterns found in sandstone

Chapter 4: Patterns and Reasoning (cont.)

Artists such as M.C. Escher use patterns in their art. A **tessellation** is a repeating pattern of interlocking shapes. **Mosaics** are pictures created by embedding small pieces of glass, stone, terracotta, etc., into cement or other fixatives. Patterns used in art also include designs in quilts and carpets.

Tessellations - Art of M.C. Escher

Mosaics

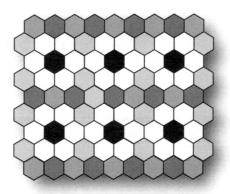

Quilt Patterns

Chapter 4: Patterns and Reasoning (cont.)

❷ The Structure of Geometry

Geometry is guided by the rules of geometry. To prove a new rule, you must use at least one other rule. Some rules for the study of geometry are called **postulates** or **axioms** that must be accepted without proving them to be true. Once you know the postulates, you can develop new rules called **theorems**. When reading geometry books, you might find that not every book uses the same postulates or axioms.

Postulate One, the ruler postulate, states that the points on a line can be matched, one-to-one, with the set of real numbers. A real number that corresponds with a point is the coordinate of that point. The distance $\overline{AB}$ between the two points A and B on a line is equal to the absolute value of the difference between the coordinates of A and B. **Postulate Two**, the segment addition postulate, states that if B is between A and C, then $\overline{AB} + \overline{BC} = \overline{AC}$.

Example of Postulate One using an inch scale: $\overline{AB} = |\,6 - 3\,| = 3$ inches

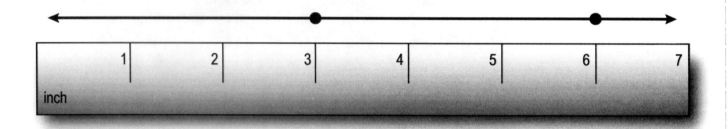

Example of Postulate One using a different scale (cm): $\overline{AB} = |\,15.2 - 7.6\,| = 7.6$ cm

Using a different scale, the distance would not be the same.

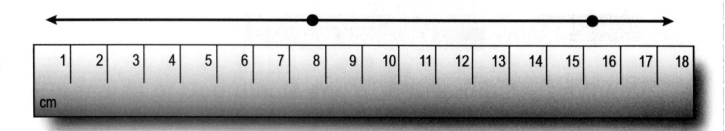

Chapter 4: Patterns and Reasoning (cont.)

Example of Postulate Two: If B is between A and C, then $\overline{AB} + \overline{BC} = \overline{AC}$.

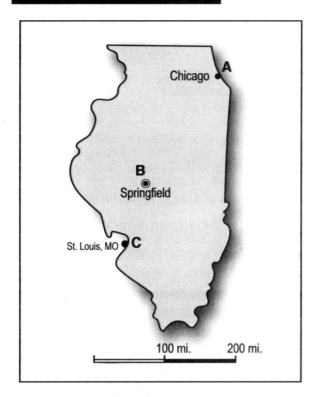

Find the distance from Chicago, IL, to St. Louis, MO. ($\overline{AC}$).

The scale for this map is approximately 1 cm/100 miles.

The distance from Chicago to Springfield ≈ 2 cm, so $\overline{AB}$ = 200 miles.

The distance from Springfield to St. Louis, MO ≈ 1 cm, so $\overline{BC}$ = 100 miles.

Springfield is between Chicago and St. Louis, so $\overline{AC} = \overline{AB} + \overline{BC}$.
$\overline{AC}$ = 200 + 100 = 300 miles.

Postulate Three: The protractor postulate states that the rays of the form $\overrightarrow{OD}$ where D is in the half-plane P, can be put in one-to-one correspondence with the real numbers between 0° and 180° inclusive. Note that the plane in the example below is divided by $\overrightarrow{OD}$. It may help to think of a plane as a whole sheet of paper versus the half-plane that is part of the sheet of paper. Point O or A or $\overrightarrow{OA}$ is not in the half-plane P. $\overrightarrow{OD}$ and $\overrightarrow{OC}$ and the points C and D are all in the half-plane P. If C and D are in the half-plane P, then the measure of the ∠COD is equal to the absolute value of the difference between the real numbers for m∠AOC and m∠AOD.

Example of Postulate Three – Protractor Postulate:

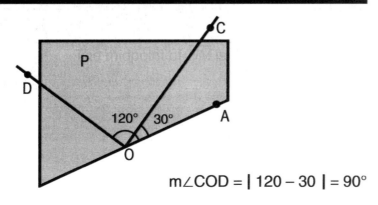

m∠COD = | 120 − 30 | = 90°

Chapter 4: Patterns and Reasoning (cont.)

❸ Angle Addition Postulate

Postulate Four: The angle addition postulate states that if *B* is in the interior of ∠AOC, then m∠AOB + m∠BOC = m∠AOC.

Example of Postulate Four – Angle Addition Postulate:

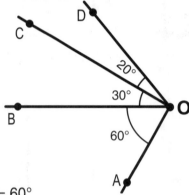

m∠AOC = 90°, m∠AOB = 60°

Find m∠BOC: m∠AOC = m∠AOB + m∠BOC

Substitute the known measures: 90° = 60° + m∠BOC

Solve: 90° − 60° = 60° − 60° + m∠BOC

30° = m∠BOC

Postulate Five states that through any two distinct points there exists exactly one line. **Postulate Six** states that a line contains at least two points. **Postulate Seven** states that through any three non-collinear points, there is exactly one plane. **Postulate Eight** states that a plane contains at least three non-collinear points. **Postulate Nine** states that if two distinct points lie in a plane, then the line containing them lies in the plane. **Postulate Ten** states that if two distinct planes intersect, then their intersection is a line.

Example of Postulate Five:

If *A* and *B* are two distinct points, then there is only one line that will pass through both points.

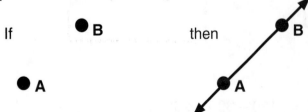

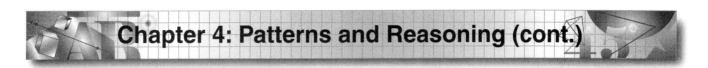

Chapter 4: Patterns and Reasoning (cont.)

Example of Postulate Six:

A line has to have at least two points. If there is only one point, then it is a point, and not a line.

Example of Postulate Seven:

If there are three non-linear points, then there is only one plane.

If   then

Example of Postulate Eight:

A plane contains at least three non-linear points.

If   then

Example of Postulate Nine:

If two points lie in a plane, then the line connecting the points is on the plane.

If   then

Chapter 4: Patterns and Reasoning (cont.)

Example of Postulate Ten:

If two planes intersect, then the intersection is a line.

If    then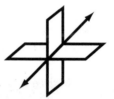

You can think of this as where two walls come together in a room or where the wall and floor meet.

❹ Conditional Statements

Some of the postulates above are stated as **conditional statements**. A conditional statement, or **if-then statement**, has two parts: the hypothesis and the conclusion. The conditional statement is if the hypothesis (p) is true, then the conclusion (q) is true. In other words, if p then q, also written as $p \Rightarrow q$. By exchanging the hypothesis and conclusion, a converse of a conditional statement is formed. The converse of the conditional statement of: if p then q is changed to: if q then p or ($q \Rightarrow p$). **Bi-conditional statements** are in the form of p if and only if q or ($p \Leftrightarrow q$). A bi-conditional is the same as writing the conditional statement and the converse simultaneously.

❺ Deductive Reasoning

Once you know the postulates, you can develop new rules called **theorems**. Geometry uses conjectures or inferences based on inclusive evidence to create new theorems. Once the theorems are developed from the conjectures, they are verified using logical or deductive reasoning. Below are examples of theorems.

- **The theorem of complementary angles** states that if two angles are both complementary to a third angle, then the measures of the two angles are equal.

- The definition of supplementary angles states that if two angles form a straight line, then the angles are supplementary. The **theorem of supplementary angles** states that if two angles are both supplementary to a third angle, then the measures of the two angles are equal.

- The definition of vertical angles is two angles where their rays form two pairs of opposite rays. The **theorem of vertical angles** states that if two angles are vertical angles, then they are congruent.

Chapter 4: Patterns and Reasoning (cont.)

Example of the Vertical Angles Theorem:

Proof: Use the figure to the right.

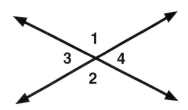

Given: $\angle 1$ and $\angle 2$ are vertical angles.

Prove: $\angle 1 \cong \angle 2$

Because $\angle 1$ and $\angle 3$ form a linear pair, they are supplementary angles, or angles the sum of which is 180°.

The measure of $\angle 1$ + the measure of $\angle 3$ = 180°.

Because $\angle 2$ and $\angle 3$ form a linear pair, they are supplementary angles. Because $\angle 1$ and $\angle 2$ are each supplementary to $\angle 3$, they must be congruent (based on the Congruent Supplements Theorem of Supplementary Angles).

Date: _____

Practice: Patterns and Reasoning/Structure of Geometry

Directions: Draw the next pattern in the sequence.

1. 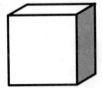   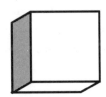   _____

2. 01   011   0112   01123   011235   _____

3.   _____

Directions: Match the postulate number in the first column with the statement in the second column.

_____ **4.** Postulate 1

_____ **5.** Postulate 2

_____ **6.** Postulate 3

_____ **7.** Postulate 4

_____ **8.** Postulate 5

_____ **9.** Postulate 6

_____ **10.** Postulate 7

_____ **11.** Postulate 8

_____ **12.** Postulate 9

_____ **13.** Postulate 10

a. If two distinct points lie in a plane, then the line containing them is also in the plane.

b. Through any two points, there is exactly one line that passes through both.

c. If two distinct planes intersect, then the intersection is a line.

d. A plane contains at least three non-linear points.

e. Through any three non-linear points, there is exactly one plane.

f. A line contains at least two points.

g. Points on a line can be matched one-to-one with a set of real numbers.

h. If B is between A and C, then $\overline{AB} + \overline{BC} = \overline{AC}$.

i. $\overrightarrow{OA}$ is a ray; P is a half-plane. Rays of the form $\overrightarrow{OD}$ where D is in P can be put in a one-to-one correspondence with the real numbers between 0 and 180 inclusive.

j. If C is in the interior of ∠AOD, then m∠AOC + m∠COD = m∠AOD.

Chapter 4: Patterns and Reasoning (cont.)

Summary of Patterns and Reasoning

Reasoning in geometry usually consists of three parts: inductive reasoning to look for patterns, making conjectures, and verifying the conjectures made using logical reasoning.

Geometry is guided by the rules of geometry. Some rules for the study of geometry are called postulates or axioms and must be accepted as true without proof. Once you know the postulates, you can develop new rules called theorems. To prove a new rule, you must use at least one other rule.

Tips to Remember for Patterns and Reasoning in Geometry

Patterns can often have more than one way to be explained. So not only is it important to extend a pattern, but to explain your choice. Geometry often models ideas in life, so be aware of your surroundings to see the geometry relationships around you. Definitions, postulates, theorems, and axioms are all ways we know that relationships in geometry are true. You can always use rules that you know are true to prove new rules.

Real Life Applications of Patterns and Reasoning in Geometry

Patterns were used in determining the number of blocks in each layer when constructing pyramids in Egypt.

Engineers use geometry to design and construct support structures in buildings, bridges, and highways. Pilots of boats, planes, and spaceships use geometry to navigate. Armed forces need to know geometry to navigate and to fire missiles and guns. Geometry is used in putting in shelves, figuring out how much gravel is needed for a road, or making patterns for clothes.

The segment addition postulate can be used to determine distance on a map, even though all roads are not "straight lines."

Chapter 5: Triangles

Introduction to the Concepts of Triangles

Polygons are closed figures with three or more sides that lie in a single plane. The sides of a polygon are called **line segments**. The sides of the polygon intersect at the **endpoints**, or **vertices**. The polygon with the fewest sides is a triangle. This section of the worktext will introduce different types of triangles.

Concepts of Triangles

1 Interior and Exterior Angles of a Triangle

2 Types of Triangles

3 Parts of a Triangle

4 Similar and Congruent Triangles

5 Properties of Triangles

6 Perimeter and Area of a Triangle

Explanations of the Concepts of Triangles

1 **Interior and Exterior Angles of a Triangle**

The **interior angles** of a triangle are all less than 180°. In the sample below, the vertices are at points A, B, and C. The three sides are $\overline{AB}$, $\overline{AC}$, and $\overline{BC}$. The interior angles are the angles at the vertices ∠ABC, ∠BCA, and ∠CAB.

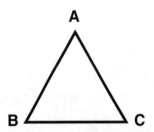

An **exterior angle** forms a straight line with the interior angle. Extending the side of a triangle past the vertex forms an exterior angle. In the triangle in Figure 1 below, ∠2 is an exterior angle.

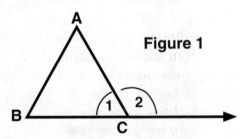

Figure 1

Chapter 5: Triangles (cont.)

Figure 2 shows that extending two sides from ∠1 forms two exterior angles, ∠2 and ∠3, and a vertical angle, ∠4. Every triangle has six possible exterior angles, two at each vertex, that are formed by extending the sides.

Figure 2

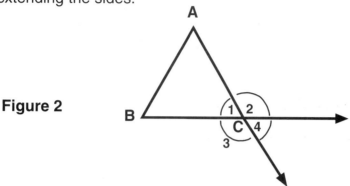

There are four theorems related to the interior and exterior angles of a triangle. These theorems include:

Theorems for the Interior Angles of a Triangle

- Every angle of a triangle has a measure greater than 0 and less than 180°.
- The sum of the measures of the angles of a triangle is 180°.

Theorems for the Exterior Angles of a Triangle

- The measure of an exterior angle of a triangle is equal to the sum of the measures of the two non-adjacent interior angles.
- The measure of any exterior angle of a triangle is greater than the measure of either of the two non-adjacent interior angles.

❷ Types of Triangles

Triangles are named by the size of the angles making the triangle. Some types of triangles include acute, obtuse, right, isosceles, equilateral, and scalene. An **acute triangle** is a triangle in which all of the interior angles are less than 90°. That means that every angle of an acute triangle is an acute angle. An **obtuse triangle** is a triangle with one obtuse angle. Remember that an obtuse angle is greater than 90°. A **right triangle** is a triangle with one right angle, which measures 90°. An **isosceles triangle** is a triangle with two congruent angles and two congruent sides. Remember that if angles or sides are congruent, they must have exactly the same measurement. An **equilateral triangle** is a triangle with three equal sides and three equal angles. A **scalene triangle** is a triangle with no congruent sides or angles. This means that all of the sides and angles have different measures. A scalene triangle can be an acute, obtuse, or right triangle.

Chapter 5: Triangles (cont.)

Examples of acute triangles: (All angles measures less than 90°.

 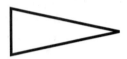

Examples of obtuse triangles: (One angle measures more than 90°.)

Examples of right triangles: (One angle equals 90°.)

 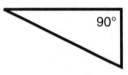

Examples of isosceles triangles: (Two sides are equal.)

Examples of equilateral triangles: (All sides are equal, and all angles are equal. This is also an equiangular triangle)

Example of a scalene triangle: (No sides are equal.)

Chapter 5: Triangles (cont.)

❸ Parts of a Triangle

Triangles have three sides and three angles. There are special names given to the angles and sides of the triangle based on their relationship to each other. The words **adjacent, opposite,** and **included** are used to refer to these relationships.

Examples of names used to show the relationships of the angles and sides:

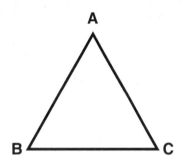

Sides $\overline{AB}$ and $\overline{AC}$ are both **adjacent** to ∠A.
Sides $\overline{BC}$ and $\overline{BA}$ are both **adjacent** to ∠B.
Sides $\overline{CA}$ and $\overline{CB}$ are both **adjacent** to ∠C.

Side $\overline{AB}$ is **included** between ∠A and ∠B.
Side $\overline{AC}$ is **included** between ∠A and ∠C.
Side $\overline{BC}$ is **included** between ∠B and ∠C.

∠A is **included** between sides $\overline{AB}$ and $\overline{AC}$.
∠B is **included** between sides $\overline{AB}$ and $\overline{BC}$.
∠C is **included** between sides $\overline{BC}$ and $\overline{AC}$.

Side $\overline{BC}$ is **opposite** ∠A.
Side $\overline{AB}$ is **opposite** ∠C.
Side $\overline{AC}$ is **opposite** ∠B.

❹ Similar and Congruent Triangles

Understanding all of the parts of a triangle leads to the discussion of similar, congruent, and congruent right triangles. If two triangles are **similar**, then they have these characteristics: the three angles are congruent or equal, respectively, to the three corresponding angles of the other triangle; and the two corresponding sides of one triangle are equal to the ratio of the two corresponding sides of the other triangle. We often say that similar triangles look like each other.

Chapter 5: Triangles (cont.)

Examples of similar triangles:

Congruent triangles have the same size and shape, which means the angles and sides of one triangle are congruent to the corresponding angles and sides of the other triangle. The following are geometric postulates related to congruency. The **SSS postulate** states that if three sides of one triangle are congruent to the three sides of another triangle, then the triangles are congruent. The **SAS postulate** states that if two sides and the included angle of one triangle are congruent to two sides and the included angle of a second triangle, then the triangles are congruent. The **ASA** postulate states that if two angles and the included side of one triangle are congruent to two angles and the included side of another triangle, then the two triangles are congruent. The **AAS postulate** states that two triangles are congruent if two angles and the side opposite one of them in the triangle are congruent to the angles and the side opposite in the other triangle. Sometimes only one of these is listed as a postulate, and the others are proven as theorems. In any case, all four are considered true statements.

Examples of congruent triangles:

Other congruent triangles are congruent right triangles. A **right triangle** is a triangle that has one 90° angle. The side opposite the right angle is called the **hypotenuse**. The hypotenuse is a diagonal line that connects the other two sides of the triangle. The other two sides are called the **legs** of the triangle. The **Hypotenuse-Leg Postulate** states that two right triangles are congruent if the hypotenuse and leg of one right triangle are congruent to the hypotenuse and leg of another right triangle. The **Leg-Leg Postulate** states that two right triangles are congruent if the legs of one right triangle are congruent to the legs of another right triangle. The **Hypotenuse-Acute Angle Postulate** states that two right triangles are congruent if the hypotenuse and an acute angle of one right triangle are congruent to the hypotenuse and acute angle of the other right triangle.

Chapter 5: Triangles (cont.)

Examples of congruent right triangles:

⑤ Properties of Triangles

The **Pythagorean Theorem** states that the square of the length of the hypotenuse of a right triangle is equal to the sum of the squares of the lengths of the legs. You can determine the length of any side of a right triangle if you know the lengths of the other two sides. According to the Pythagorean Theorem, the square of the length of one of the legs (s_1) plus the square of the length of the second leg (s_2) is equal to the square of the length of the hypotenuse (h). So the equation could be represented by $s_1^2 + s_2^2 = h^2$. Sometimes you will see this written in the form $a^2 + b^2 = c^2$, where a and b are the lengths of the legs, and c is the length of the hypotenuse.

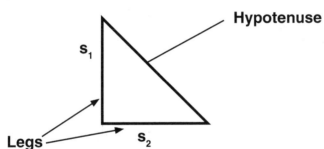

Examples of the Pythagorean Theorem:

Problem: Find the hypotenuse of the right triangle if you know the length of the legs.

$$s_1 = 2 \text{ cm} \qquad s_2 = 3 \text{ cm}$$

Step 1:   Substitute the numbers for the legs in the theorem. $s_1^2 + s_2^2 = h^2$

$$(2)^2 + (3)^2 = h^2$$

Step 2:   Solve: $\sqrt{4 + 9} = \sqrt{h^2}$

Answer: $\sqrt{13} \text{ cm} = h$

Chapter 5: Triangles (cont.)

Problem: Find the leg of the right triangle if you know the length of one leg and the hypotenuse.

$s_2 = 6$ cm $10 = h$ $s_1 = ?$

Step 1:   Substitute the numbers for the length of the leg and the hypotenuse in the theorem. $s_1^2 + s_2^2 = h^2$

$s_1^2 + (6)^2 = (10)^2$

Step 2:   Solve: $s_1^2 + 36 = 100$

$s_1^2 + 36 - 36 = 100 - 36$

$s_1^2 = 64$

$\sqrt{s_1^2} = \sqrt{64}$

Answer: $s_1 = 8$

The **Mid-Segment Theorem** states that the segment connecting the midpoints of two sides of a triangle is parallel to the third side and is half its length. Remember from the coordinate chapter that the midpoint of a line can be found using the midpoint formula: let $A(x_1, y_1)$ and $B(x_2, y_2)$ be points in a coordinate plane. The midpoint of $\overline{AB}$ is $\left(\dfrac{x_1 + x_2}{2}, \dfrac{y_1 + y_2}{2}\right)$. Also, remember that the formula for finding the slope of a line is $\dfrac{rise}{run} = \dfrac{y_2 - y_1}{x_2 - x_1}$.

Example of finding the mid-segments of a triangle:

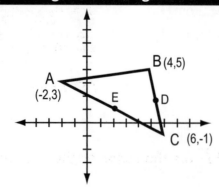

Chapter 5: Triangles (cont.)

Problem: Find the midpoint of $\overline{BC}$ labeled D and the midpoint of $\overline{AC}$ labeled E on the drawing on the previous page.

Step 1: Midpoint of $\overline{BC} = \left(\dfrac{x_1 + x_2}{2}, \dfrac{y_1 + y_2}{2}\right)$ Midpoint of $\overline{AC} = \left(\dfrac{x_1 + x_2}{2}, \dfrac{y_1 + y_2}{2}\right)$

Step 2: Midpoint of $\overline{BC} = \left(\dfrac{4 + 6}{2}, \dfrac{5 + (-1)}{2}\right)$ Midpoint of $\overline{AC} = \left(\dfrac{6 + (-2)}{2}, \dfrac{-1 + 3}{2}\right)$

Step 3: Midpoint of $\overline{BC} = \left(\dfrac{10}{2}, \dfrac{4}{2}\right) = (5, 2)$ Midpoint of $\overline{AC} = \left(\dfrac{4}{2}, \dfrac{2}{2}\right) = (2, 1)$

Answers: Coordinates of the midpoint D are (5, 2).   Coordinates of the midpoint E are (2, 1).

Example of the mid-segment theorem of a triangle:

Problem: Using the midpoints in triangle ABC above, draw segment $\overline{ED}$.

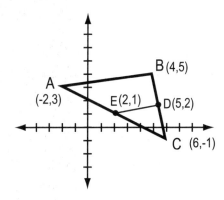

Step 1: Find the slopes of $\overline{AB}$ and $\overline{ED}$.

$$m = \dfrac{rise}{run} = \dfrac{y_2 - y_1}{x_2 - x_1}$$ $$m = \dfrac{rise}{run} = \dfrac{y_2 - y_1}{x_2 - x_1}$$

Step 2: $\overline{AB}\ m = \dfrac{5 - 3}{4 - (-2)}$ $\overline{ED}\ m = \dfrac{2 - 1}{5 - 2}$

Step 3: $\overline{AB}\ m = \dfrac{2}{6} = \dfrac{1}{3}$ $\overline{ED}\ m = \dfrac{1}{3}$

Answer: The slopes of $\overline{AB}$ and $\overline{ED}$ are the same, so the lines are parallel.

Chapter 5: Triangles (cont.)

Triangles have special segments that include: perpendicular bisectors, angle bisectors, medians, and altitudes. An **angle bisector** is a ray that divides an angle into two equal parts, and these were discussed previously in the chapter on angles. A **perpendicular bisector** of a segment is a line that is perpendicular to the segment at its midpoint. A **median** is a segment whose endpoints are a vertex and the midpoint of the opposite side. The perpendicular bisector, angle bisector, and median are in a triangle's interior. An **altitude** is a segment from a vertex that is perpendicular to the opposite side or to the line containing the opposite side. An altitude may be inside or outside a triangle. Notice that angle bisectors, medians, and altitudes always have one endpoint that is a **vertex**. The perpendicular bisector is a line, and it may or may not contain a vertex of the triangle.

Example of a perpendicular bisector of a triangle:

Problem: Find the midpoint of $\overline{AC}$ labeled D on the drawing.

Step 1:   Midpoint of $\overline{AC} = \left(\dfrac{0 + 10}{2}, \dfrac{0 + 0}{2} \right)$

Step 2:   Midpoint of $\overline{AC} = \left(\dfrac{10}{2}, \dfrac{0}{2} \right) = (5, 0)$

The midpoint D has the coordinates of (5, 0).

Step 3:   Using a protractor, draw a perpendicular line from the point to line $\overline{BC}$.

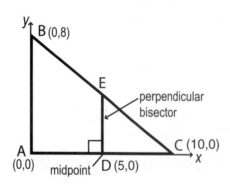

 **Chapter 5: Triangles (cont.)**

Example of an angle bisector of a triangle:

Angle DEF is 90°.

Half of 90 = 45, so the bisector angle is 45°.

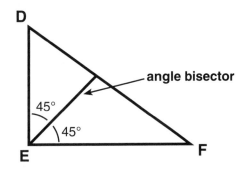

Example of a median of a triangle:

Problem: Find the midpoint of $\overline{GI}$ labeled J in the drawing.

Midpoint of $\overline{GI} = \left(\dfrac{x_1 + x_2}{2}, \dfrac{y_1 + y_2}{2}\right)$

Step 1: Midpoint of $\overline{GI} = \left(\dfrac{0 + 10}{2}, \dfrac{0 + 0}{2}\right)$

Step 2: Midpoint of $\overline{GI} = \left(\dfrac{10}{2}, \dfrac{0}{2}\right) = (5, 0)$

The coordinates of the midpoint J are (5, 0).

Step 3: Draw a line from the midpoint (J) to the vertex (H) of ∠GHI.

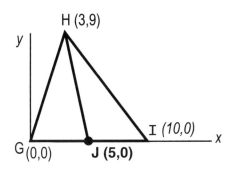

Chapter 5: Triangles (cont.)

Example of an altitude of a triangle:

Using a protractor, draw a perpendicular line from the vertex of $\angle$KLM to $\overline{KM}$.

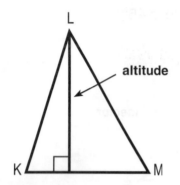

In examining the angles and sides of a triangle, **two other theorems** apply: (1) If one side of a triangle is longer than another side, then the angle opposite the longer side will be larger than the angle opposite the shorter side. If one angle of a triangle is larger than another angle, then the side opposite the larger angle is longer than the side opposite the smaller angle. (2) The **triangle inequality theorem** states that the sum of the lengths of any two sides (s_1 and s_2) of a triangle is greater than the length of the third side (s_3). This can be represented by the equation: $s_1 + s_2 > s_3$.

Examples of triangle inequality:

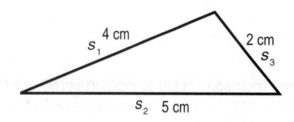

$s_1 + s_2 > s_3$	$s_1 + s_3 > s_2$	$s_2 + s_3 > s_1$
$4 + 5 > 2$	$4 + 2 > 5$	$5 + 2 > 4$

Chapter 5: Triangles (cont.)

⑥ Perimeter and Area of a Triangle

The perimeter of a triangle is the distance around the triangle. It can be found by finding the sum of the lengths of all three sides. We can represent this by the equation $p = s_1 + s_2 + s_3$.

Example of finding the perimeter of a triangle:

Problem: $\overline{AB} = 1.5$ cm, $\overline{BC} = 5$ cm, $\overline{CA} = 4$ cm

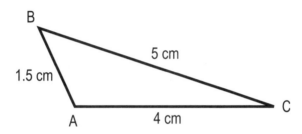

$p = s_1 + s_2 + s_3$

Step 1: Substitute the numbers for the lengths of the sides in the equation.

$p = 1.5 + 5 + 4$

Step 2: $p = 10.5$ cm

Answer: The perimeter is 10.5 cm.

The **area of a polygon** can be thought of as the number of square units contained in the interior. The **area of a triangle** can be found by multiplying one-half the base times the height of the altitude. This is written as $A = \frac{1}{2}(bh)$, where A represents the area, b represents the base, and h represents the height of the altitude. Remember that the altitude is the line segment from the vertex of the triangle perpendicular to the opposite side, or the opposite side extended. Each triangle has three angles, so it has three altitudes. The answer is given in square units—for example, square inches, square centimeters, or square units.

Chapter 5: Triangles (cont.)

Example of finding the area of a triangle:

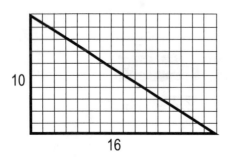

10

16

Each square on the grid represents one centimeter.

Problem: Base = 16 cm and altitude = 10 cm

$A = \frac{1}{2}(bh)$

Step 1:   Substitute the numbers of the base and height of the altitude in the equation.

$A = \frac{1}{2}(16 \times 10)$

Step 2: $A = \frac{1}{2}(160)$

$A = 80$

Step 3:   Add the units. In this case, the units are square centimeters.

Answer: $A = 80 \text{ cm}^2$

Name: _____ Date: _____

Chapter 5: Triangles (cont.)

Practice: Triangles

Directions: Match the triangle with its name and explain why it is that type of triangle. Some answers will be used more than once.

a.

b.

c.

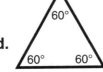

d.

e.

_____ **1.** Acute

This is an acute triangle because_____

_____

_____ **2.** Obtuse

This is an obtuse triangle because _____

_____

_____ **3.** Right triangle

This is a right triangle because _____

_____

_____ **4.** Isosceles

This is an isosceles triangle because _____

_____

_____ **5.** Equilateral

This is an equilateral triangle because _____

_____

_____ **6.** Equiangular

This is an equiangular triangle because _____

_____

_____ **7.** Scalene

This is a scalene triangle because _____

_____

me: _____ Date: _____

Chapter 5: Triangles (cont.)

Directions: Use the Pythagorean Theorem to solve problems 8–9.

8. Find the hypotenuse of the right triangle ABC.
   $s_1 = 5$ cm and $s_2 = 3$ cm

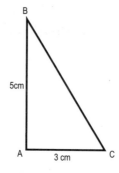

9. Find the leg of the right triangle DEF. $s_2 = 5$ cm and $h = 7$ cm
   $s_1^2 + s_2^2 = h^2$

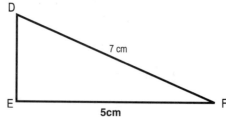

Special Segments

10. Find the perpendicular bisector of the segment $\overline{AC}$.
    Find the midpoint of $\overline{AC}$ and label the point D.
    Using a protractor, draw a perpendicular line from
    point D to line $\overline{BC}$.

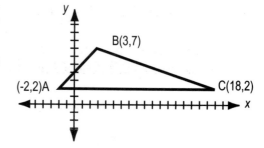

11. Find the angle bisector of $\angle ABC$.

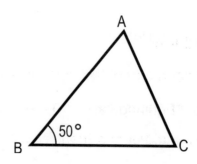

Name: _____ Date: _____

Chapter 5: Triangles (cont.)

12. Find the median of the triangle DEF for ∠E.
Find the midpoint of $\overline{DF}$ and label it G.
Draw a line from the midpoint (G) to the vertex of ∠DEF.

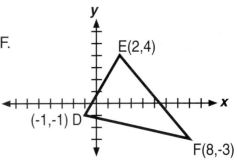

13. Find the altitude of the triangle NOP for ∠O.
Draw a perpendicular line from the vertex
of angle NOP for $\overline{NP}$.

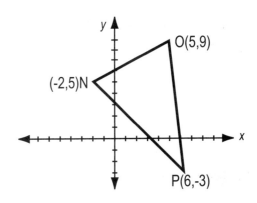

Directions: Use the mid-segment theorem.

14. Show that the segment formed by midpoint J
of $\overline{LM}$ and the midpoint I of $\overline{KM}$ is parallel to $\overline{KL}$.

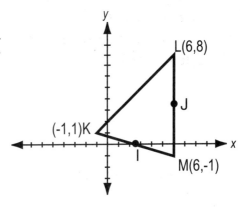

Perimeter and Area

15. Find the perimeter of the triangle with sides of 5 cm, 4 cm, and 7 cm. _____

16. Find the perimeter of a triangle with the sides of 4 cm, 15 cm, and 9 cm. _____

17. Find the perimeter of a triangle with the sides of 5.5 cm, 7.5 cm, 3 cm. _____

18. Find the area of a triangle with a base of 8 cm and an altitude of 5 cm. _____

19. Find the area of a triangle with a base of 10 cm and an altitude of 7 cm. _____

20. Find the area of a triangle with a base of 15 cm and an altitude of 4 cm. _____

Chapter 5: Triangles (cont.)

Summary of Triangles

Each of the three interior angles of a triangle is less than 180°. Extending the side of a triangle past the vertex forms an exterior angle. An exterior angle forms a straight line with the interior angle. A triangle has six exterior angles.

Theorems for the interior angles of a triangle state: every angle of a triangle has a measure greater than 0 and less than 180°, and the sum of the measures of the angles of a triangle is 180°. Theorems for exterior angles of triangles include: the measure of an exterior angle of a triangle is equal to the sum of the measures of the two non-adjacent interior angles, and the measure of any exterior angle of a triangle is greater than the measure of either of the two non-adjacent interior angles.

Triangles are named by the size of the angles making the triangle. Some types of triangles include acute, obtuse, right, isosceles, equilateral, and scalene. Two triangles are similar if the three angles of one are equal in measure to the three angles of the other. Congruent triangles have the same size and shape, which means that the angles and sides are congruent, or the same measure. Triangles have special segments, or lines, that include: perpendicular bisectors, angle bisectors, medians, and altitudes.

Important Theorems:

- The **Pythagorean Theorem** states that the square of the length of the hypotenuse of a right triangle is equal to the sum of the squares of the lengths of the legs.
- The **Mid-Segment Theorem** states that the segment connecting the midpoints of two sides of a triangle is parallel to the third side and is half its length.
- The **Triangle Inequality Theorem** states that the sum of the lengths of any two sides (s_1 and s_2) of a triangle is greater than the length of the third side (s_3).

Tips to Remember for Triangles

Within the set of triangles, there are many classification systems that you should remember, such as acute, obtuse, right, isosceles, equilateral, and scalene. Pay special attention to the meaning of each.

When working with triangles, keep in mind the properties, rules, theorems, and the relationships they are describing. Knowing one piece of information may allow you to make inferences about other pieces of information. For example, knowing that an isosceles triangle is a triangle with two sides of equal length allows us to infer that it also has two angles of equal measure. Also, knowing that an exterior angle of a triangle is equal to the sum of two non-adjacent interior angles allows us to infer that the exterior angle must have a greater measure than either non-adjacent interior angle.

Some of the special lines and line segments are used in other situations. The midpoint theorems are related to medians, and altitudes are used when finding the areas of triangles.

Chapter 5: Triangles (cont.)

Real Life Applications of Triangles

Triangles can be considered "building blocks." A triangle is a rigid structure, so constructing buildings with triangles can make the building stronger. Isosceles triangles can be seen in the rafters of a house or the supports of a tepee.

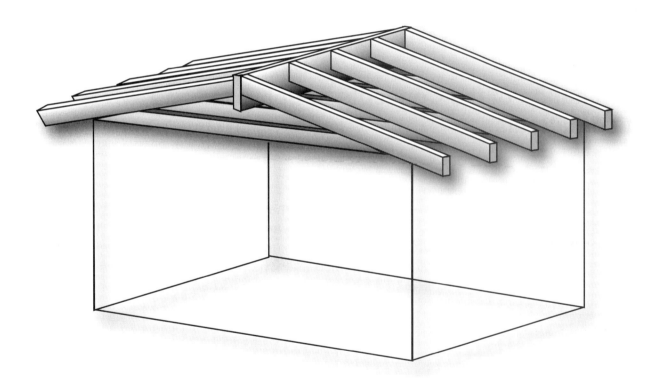

Introduction to the Concepts of Polygons and Quadrilaterals

In the introductory chapter, polygons were identified by their shapes and number of sides. Triangles have three sides, quadrilaterals have four sides, pentagons have five sides, hexagons have six sides, and octagons have eight sides. A polygon must be in one plane. This section will focus on four-sided polygons called quadrilaterals and their properties. A square, rectangle, parallelogram, rhombus, and trapezoid are examples of quadrilaterals.

Concepts of Polygons and Quadrilaterals

1 Polygons

2 Quadrilaterals

Explanation of the Concepts of Polygons and Quadrilaterals

1 **Polygons**

Poly is a prefix that means "more than one, or many." *Gon* is a word that means "angle." So a polygon has many angles. A polygon has the same number of sides as it has angles. **Polygons** are plane figures that are formed by three or more line segments called **sides**. Each side of a polygon intersects two other sides, once at each endpoint. No two sides of a polygon with a common endpoint are collinear. As discussed earlier, **collinear** means that the points are on the same line.

Examples of polygons:

A polygon is **convex** if no line that contains a side of the polygon contains an interior point.

Examples of convex polygons:

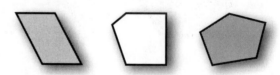

Chapter 6: Polygons and Quadrilaterals (cont.)

A polygon that is not convex is called a **non-convex**, or a **concave** polygon.

Examples of non-convex or concave polygons:

By definition, a polygon must have at least three sides. The polygon with the fewest number of sides is a triangle with three sides. Polygons have vertices, interior angles, exterior angles, perimeter, and area. Polygons also have diagonal segments that join two nonconsecutive vertices. A polygon is **equilateral** if all sides are congruent. It is **equiangular** if all interior angles are congruent. A polygon that is equilateral and equiangular is **regular.** That is, all angles and sides are congruent. A **diagonal** of a polygon is a line segment joining non-adjacent vertices.

Examples of diagonal segments in polygons:

In *Figure 1*, $\overline{BD}$ and $\overline{AC}$ are diagonals.

In *Figure 2*, $\overline{AC}$, $\overline{AD}$, and $\overline{AE}$ are diagonals.

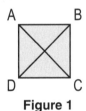

Figure 1   Figure 2

Examples of equilateral polygons:

 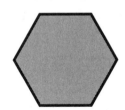 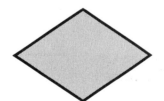 

Examples of equiangular polygons:

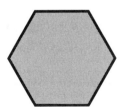  

Chapter 6: Polygons and Quadrilaterals (cont.)

Examples of regular polygons:

The sum of the interior angles of polygons can be determined by using the **polygon interior angles theorem**. This theorem states that the sum of the measures of the interior angles of a convex n-gon (n representing the number of sides) is $(n-2)(180°)$. The sum of the interior angles in a triangle is 180°, so if you count the number of triangles that can be used to partition a polygon into non-overlapping triangles and multiply it by 180°, you will obtain the sum of the interior angles in the polygon. Based on the theorem above, the number of triangles made inside the polygon by drawing all diagonals from one vertex is represented by the number of sides minus two. Notice that the prefix tells you the number of sides in each of the polygons. For example, the word triangle has the prefix *tri-*, which means "three," and it has three sides; *quad* is a prefix meaning "four," and it has four sides.

Examples of finding the sum of the measure of the interior angles of a polygon:

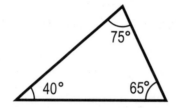

The triangle has three sides, and the angles total 180°. $(3-2)(180°) = 180°$

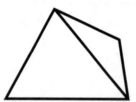

The quadrilateral can be divided into two triangles. $(4-2)(180°) = 360°$

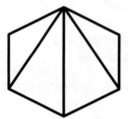

The hexagon can be divided into four triangles. $(6-2)(180°) = 720°$

The table below shows the sum of the interior angles for sample polygons. The final row shows the formula used with any polygon. Note that the number of sides minus 2 gives the number of triangles that can be used to partition the polygon.

Chapter 6: Polygons and Quadrilaterals (cont.)

Polygon	Number of Sides *(n)*	Number of Triangles	Sum of Interior Angles
Triangle	3	1	1(180°) = 180°
Quadrilateral	4	2	2(180°) = 360°
Pentagon	5	3	3(180°) = 540°
Hexagon	6	4	4(180°) = 720°
Heptagon	7	5	5(180°) = 900°
Octagon	8	6	6(180°) = 1,080°
n-gon	*n*	*n* – 2	(*n* – 2)(180°)

All angles of a regular polygon are congruent. The **corollary theorem**, as related to polygons, states that the measure of each interior angle of a regular *n*-gon is $\frac{1}{n}(n-2)(180°)$. That is, take the sum of the interior angles (*n* – 2)(180°) and divide by the number of vertices/angles. The table below shows the measure of some regular polygon interior angles.

Regular Polygon	Number of Sides *(n)*	Measure of Interior Angle $\frac{1}{n}(n-2)(180°)$
Triangle	3	$\frac{1}{3}(3-2) = \frac{1}{3}(180°) = 60°$
Square	4	$\frac{1}{4}(4-2)(180°) = \frac{1}{4}(2)(180°) = \frac{1}{4}(360°) = 90°$
Pentagon	5	$\frac{1}{5}(5-2)(180°) = \frac{1}{5}(3)(180°) = \frac{1}{5}(540°) = 108°$
Hexagon	6	$\frac{1}{6}(6-2)(180°) = \frac{1}{6}(4)(180°) = \frac{1}{6}(720°) = 120°$
Heptagon	7	$\frac{1}{7}(7-2)(180°) = \frac{1}{7}(5)(180°) = \frac{1}{7}(900°) \approx 128.6°$
Octagon	8	$\frac{1}{8}(8-2)(180°) = \frac{1}{8}(6)(180°) = \frac{1}{8}(1{,}080°) = 135°$
n–gon	*n*	$\frac{1}{n}(n-2)(180°)$

You can find the measure of the angles of polygons that are not regular if you know some of the measures of the angles in the polygon.

Example of finding the measure of the interior angles using equations:

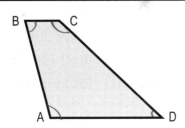

Chapter 6: Polygons and Quadrilaterals (cont.)

Problem: What are the measures of each of the angles?

If the interior angles of a quadrilateral are put in increasing order, they increase by 30°.

This is a quadrilateral, so we know the sum of all interior angles is 360°.

Step 1:   Start with $\angle D$ since it is the smallest. $\angle D = x$

The next smallest angle is $\angle B$, so $\angle B = x + 30°$

$m\angle A = x + 30° + 30° = x + 60°$

$m\angle C = x + 60° + 30° = x + 90°$

Step 2:   Put the equation together:

$x + (x + 30°) + (x + 60°) + (x + 90°) = 360°$

Step 3:   Simplify:

$4x + 180° = 360°$

$4x + 180° - 180° = 360° - 180°$

$4x = 180°$

$$\frac{4x}{4} = \frac{180°}{4}$$

$x = 45°$

Answers: $m\angle D = x = 45°$

$m\angle B = x + 30° = 45° + 30° = 75°$

$m\angle A = x + 60° = 45° + 60° = 105°$

$m\angle C = x + 90° = 45° + 90° = 135°$

To find the measure of the exterior angles of polygons, extend the sides of a convex polygon. The **polygon exterior angles theorem** states that the sum of the measures of the exterior angles, one from each vertex of a convex polygon, is equal to 360°. The corollary to this theorem states that the measure of each exterior angle of a regular n-gon is $\frac{1}{n}(360°)$.

If the sides are extended on a polygon, then the interior and exterior angles are supplementary, which means that they add up to 180°. Knowing the measure of the interior or exterior angle, the other angle can be found by subtracting the measure of the angle from 180°.

Chapter 6: Polygons and Quadrilaterals (cont.)

Example of finding the interior or exterior angles of a polygon:

$m\angle 2 = 100°$

$m\angle 8 = 40°$

$m\angle 4 = m\angle 5 = 110°$

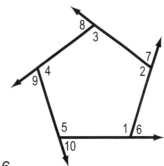

Problem: Find the measures of

$\angle 7$, $\angle 3$, $\angle 9$, $\angle 10$, $\angle 1$, and $\angle 6$.

Step 1:   Which angles are supplementary?

$\angle 2$ and $\angle 7$, $\angle 8$ and $\angle 3$, $\angle 9$ and $\angle 4$, $\angle 5$ and $\angle 10$, and $\angle 1$ and $\angle 6$

Step 2:   Supplementary angles add up to 180°. Set up equations to find these measures.

$m\angle 7 = 180° - m\angle 2$	$m\angle 3 = 180° - m\angle 8$	$m\angle 9 = 180° - m\angle 4$
$m\angle 7 = 180° - 100°$	$m\angle 3 = 180° - 40°$	$m\angle 9 = 180° - 110°$
$m\angle 7 = 80°$	$m\angle 3 = 140°$	$m\angle 9 = 70°$

$m\angle 10 = 180° - m\angle 5$

$m\angle 10 = 180° - 110°$

$m\angle 10 = 70°$

Step 3:   The sum of the interior angles of a pentagon is 540°. Subtract the measure of all of the other interior angles to find out the measure of $\angle 1$.

$m\angle 1 = 540° - m\angle 2 - m\angle 3 - m\angle 4 - m\angle 5$

$m\angle 1 = 540° - 100° - 140° - 110° - 110°$

$m\angle 1 = 80°$

Step 4: $m\angle 6$ is supplementary to $m\angle 1$.

$m\angle 6 = 180° - m\angle 1$

$m\angle 6 = 180° - 80°$

$m\angle 6 = 100°$

Chapter 6: Polygons and Quadrilaterals (cont.)

❷ Quadrilaterals

Quadrilaterals are four-sided polygons. The most common quadrilaterals are squares and rectangles. Other quadrilaterals are trapezoids, parallelograms, and rhombuses.

A **trapezoid** has one pair of parallel sides that are called bases and two non-parallel sides called legs. The **median** of a trapezoid is a line segment that connects the midpoints of the legs. It is also parallel to both bases. The length of the median is one-half the sum of the two bases, $\frac{1}{2}(b_1 + b_2)$, also written as $\frac{b_1 + b_2}{2}$, or the average of the two bases.

Examples of trapezoids:

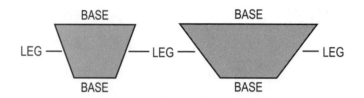

Example of finding the median of a trapezoid:

Problem: Find the median of this trapezoid.

$b_1 = 6$ $b_2 = 20$

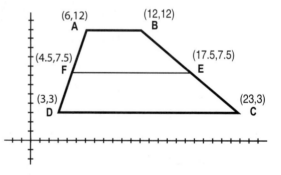

Step 1: $\dfrac{b_1 + b_2}{2}$

Step 2: $\dfrac{6 + 20}{2} = \dfrac{26}{2} = 13$

Answer: The median of trapezoid ABCD is 13 units.

The median connects both legs at their midpoints.

Problem: Find the midpoints of both legs $\overline{AD}$ and $\overline{BC}$.

$\overline{AD}$ point $F = \left(\dfrac{x_1 + x_2}{2}, \dfrac{y_1 + y_2}{2}\right)$ $\overline{BC}$ point $E = \left(\dfrac{x_1 + x_2}{2}, \dfrac{y_1 + y_2}{2}\right)$

Step 1: $\overline{AD} = \left(\dfrac{6 + 3}{2}, \dfrac{12 + 3}{2}\right)$ $\overline{BC} = \left(\dfrac{12 + 23}{2}, \dfrac{12 + 3}{2}\right)$

Step 2: $\overline{AD} = \left(\dfrac{9}{2}, \dfrac{15}{2}\right) = (4.5, 7.5)$ $\overline{BC} = \left(\dfrac{35}{2}, \dfrac{15}{2}\right) = (17.5, 7.5)$

Chapter 6: Polygons and Quadrilaterals (cont.)

Two theorems related to trapezoids are: (1) the pair of angles adjacent to a non-parallel side of the trapezoid are supplementary, and (2) there are two such pairs of angles, since there are two non-parallel sides in a trapezoid, and the sum of all four angles of a trapezoid is 360°. Remember that two angles are supplementary if their sum is 180°.

Examples of trapezoid supplementary angles:

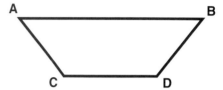

In this trapezoid, m∠A is supplementary to m∠C, and m∠B is supplementary to m∠D, so m∠A + m∠B + m∠C + m∠D = 360°.

An **isosceles trapezoid** has two legs that are equal. There are two pairs of congruent angles in an isosceles trapezoid, and the diagonals are congruent. The base angles and diagonals of an isosceles trapezoid are congruent.

Example of an isosceles trapezoid:

m∠E and m∠F are one pair of congruent base angles, and m∠D and m∠G are another pair of congruent bases of the isosceles trapezoid.

The legs of the isosceles trapezoid, $\overline{DE}$ and $\overline{FG}$, are congruent.

The diagonals of the isosceles trapezoid, $\overline{DF}$ and $\overline{EG}$, are congruent.

∠E and ∠D are supplementary because their sum is 180°.

∠G and ∠F are supplementary because their sum 180°.

Another type of quadrilateral is the **parallelogram**. A parallelogram has four sides, including two pairs of parallel sides. **Theorems related to parallelograms** include the following: the opposite sides of a parallelogram are congruent. Opposite angles of a parallelogram are also congruent. Consecutive pairs of angles of a parallelogram are supplementary. The sum of the angles of a parallelogram is 360°. Each diagonal of a parallelogram separates the parallelogram into two congruent triangles. The diagonals of a parallelogram bisect each other, and the four non-overlapping triangles formed when both diagonals are drawn are congruent.

Chapter 6: Polygons and Quadrilaterals (cont.)

Examples of parallelograms:

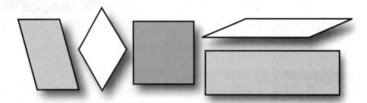

Example of the characteristics of a parallelogram:

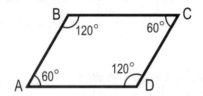

Opposite sides $\overline{AD}$ and $\overline{BC}$ are congruent, and $\overline{DC}$ and $\overline{AB}$ are congruent.

The measures of ∠B and ∠D are congruent, or are the same measure, and ∠A and ∠C are congruent.

m∠B and m∠C are supplementary (60° + 120° = 180°). ∠A and ∠D are supplementary.

Add the diagonal to the parallelogram above:

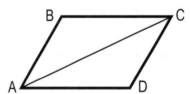

The diagonal forms two congruent triangles; △ABC is congruent to △CDA.

Add the other diagonal to the parallelogram above:

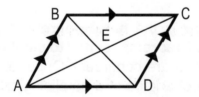

The two diagonals of the parallelogram bisect each other at point E.

Also in the figure above, arrows are used to indicate which sides are parallel and equal. The sides with one arrow are parallel and equal, and the sides with two arrows are parallel and equal.

Chapter 6: Polygons and Quadrilaterals (cont.)

A **rhombus** is also a parallelogram. They are polygons with four equal sides, and the opposite sides are parallel. **Theorems related to a rhombus** include the following: the diagonals of a rhombus bisect the angles of the rhombus, are perpendicular, separate the rhombus into two congruent triangles, and bisect each other. Opposite angles in a rhombus are congruent. Any consecutive pairs of angles are supplementary.

Examples of rhombuses:

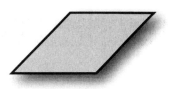

Examples of rhombuses with diagonals:

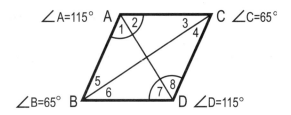

Because the diagonals bisect the angles of a rhombus:

m∠1 and m∠2 are congruent.

m∠3 and m∠4 are congruent.

m∠5 and m∠6 are congruent.

m∠7 and m∠8 are congruent.

The diagonals are perpendicular in the rhombus above.

Each individual diagonal separates the rhombus into two congruent triangles.

∠A and ∠C are supplementary because their sum is 180°.

∠B and ∠D are supplementary.

Chapter 6: Polygons and Quadrilaterals (cont.)

A **rectangle** is a parallelogram with a right angle. The **theorems related to rectangles** are: all four angles are equal, so any two angles are supplementary, and the diagonals of a rectangle separate the rectangle into two congruent triangles and bisect each other.

Examples of rectangles:

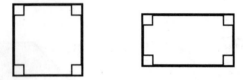

m∠A, m∠B, m∠C, and m∠D are equal to 90°, so any two angles are supplementary. $\overline{AB}$ and $\overline{CD}$ are parallel, and $\overline{BD}$ and $\overline{AC}$ are parallel.

Example of the characteristics of a rectangle:

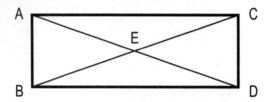

Diagonal $\overline{AD}$ separates the rectangle into two congruent triangles, ΔACD and ΔABD, and the two diagonals bisect each other at point E.

A **square** is a rectangle with four equal sides. The measures of all of the angles of a square are 90°. **Theorems related to squares** include the following: the measures of all of the angles in a square are equal. The sum of the interior angles of a square is 360°. All four sides of a square are equal. The diagonals of a square are equal, bisect each other, are perpendicular to each other, and the triangles formed by each of the diagonals are congruent.

Example of a square:

In the example on the next page, m∠D, m∠E, m∠F, and m∠G are equal to 90°. Any two angles are supplementary, and the measure of all four angles adds up to 360°.

$\overline{DE}$, $\overline{EF}$, $\overline{GF}$, and $\overline{GD}$ are all the same length.

Chapter 6: Polygons and Quadrilaterals (cont.)

Example of the characteristics of a square:

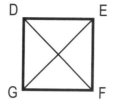

The diagonals $\overline{GE}$ and $\overline{DF}$ are equal in length, bisect each other, are perpendicular to each other, and the two triangles formed by each of the separate diagonals are congruent.

When working with geometry figures, mathematicians sometimes use symbols to identify sides and angles that are equal.

Examples of symbols used for polygons:

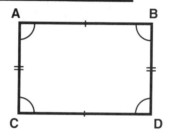

Single hash marks on $\overline{AB}$ and $\overline{CD}$ show that they are equal.

Double hash marks on $\overline{AC}$ and $\overline{BD}$ show that they are equal.

The arc shows that the m∠A, m∠B, m∠C, and m∠D are equal.

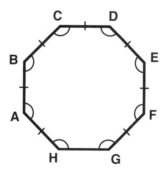

Single hash marks on all sides of the octagon show that all sides are equal.

The arc shows that all angles in the octagon are equal.

Date: _____

Chapter 6: Polygons and Quadrilaterals (cont.)

Practice: Polygons and Quadrilaterals

Directions: Identify and label the polygons found in the signs below.

1. _____

2. _____

3. _____

4. _____

5. _____

6. _____

Directions: Identify which polygon is convex and which is concave, or non-convex.

7. _____

8. _____

Directions: Using the symbols in the polygons below, identify if they are equilateral, equiangular, and/or regular polygons.

9. _____
_____
_____

10. _____
_____
_____

11. _____
_____
_____

12. _____
_____
_____

Name: _____ Date: _____

Chapter 6: Polygons and Quadrilaterals (cont.)

13. Which of the polygons in #9–12 were octagons? _____

14. Draw a regular quadrilateral.

15. Draw an equilateral hexagon that is not equiangular.

16. Find the measure of the angles using an algebraic equation. If the measures of the interior angles in a pentagon that is not regular are put in an increasing order, each differs from the next by 20°. What is the measure of each angle?

_____

17. Find m∠A. _____

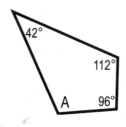

Directions: Given the measure of the angles of a regular polygon, tell how many sides each has for questions 18–20.

18. 120° _____

19. 108° _____

20. 135° _____

Directions: For questions 21–23 given the number of sides of a regular polygon, what is the measure of each angle?

21. 5 sides _____

22. 8 sides _____

23. 4 sides _____

Chapter 6: Polygons and Quadrilaterals (cont.)

Summary of Polygons and Quadrilaterals

Polygons are plane figures that are formed by three or more segments called sides. Each side of a polygon intersects two other sides, once at each endpoint. No two sides of a polygon with a common endpoint are collinear.

Polygon	Number of Sides (n)	Number of Triangles	Sum of Interior Angles
Triangle	3	1	$1(180°) = 180°$
Quadrilateral	4	2	$2(180°) = 360°$
Pentagon	5	3	$3(180°) = 540°$
Hexagon	6	4	$4(180°) = 720°$
Heptagon	7	5	$5(180°) = 900°$
Octagon	8	6	$6(180°) = 1,080°$
n-gon	n	$n - 2$	$(n - 2)(180°)$

Quadrilaterals are four-sided polygons. The most common quadrilaterals are squares and rectangles. Other quadrilaterals are trapezoids, parallelograms, and rhombuses.

Regular Polygon	Number of Sides (n)	Measure of Interior Angle $\frac{1}{n}(n-2)(180°)$
Triangle	3	$\frac{1}{3}(3-2) = \frac{1}{3}(180°) = 60°$
Square	4	$\frac{1}{4}(4-2)(180°) = \frac{1}{4}(2)(180°) = \frac{1}{4}(360°) = 90°$
Pentagon	5	$\frac{1}{5}(5-2)(180°) = \frac{1}{5}(3)(180°) = \frac{1}{5}(540°) = 108°$
Hexagon	6	$\frac{1}{6}(6-2)(180°) = \frac{1}{6}(4)(180°) = \frac{1}{6}(720°) = 120°$
Heptagon	7	$\frac{1}{7}(7-2)(180°) = \frac{1}{7}(5)(180°) = \frac{1}{7}(900°) \approx 128.6°$
Octagon	8	$\frac{1}{8}(8-2)(180°) = \frac{1}{8}(6)(180°) = \frac{1}{8}(1,080°) = 135°$
n–gon	n	$\frac{1}{n}(n-2)(180°)$

Chapter 6: Polygons and Quadrilaterals (cont.)

Tips to Remember for Polygons and Quadrilaterals

Some polygons have more than one name. For example, a square is a rectangle, a parallelogram, and a rhombus. Not all rectangles are squares, but they are parallelograms. Thus the properties for a parallelogram all hold for a rectangle as well. However, a rectangle may have extra properties.

All polygons can be partitioned into non-overlapping triangles by drawing all the diagonals from one vertex.

It is the properties of the shape, in addition to the visual appearance, that determines how various shapes are utilized.

Real Life Applications of Polygons and Quadrilaterals

Polygons and quadrilaterals are found all around us. Examples include stop signs, playing cards, buildings, computer screens, some wallpaper designs, pictures, and architecture. Triangles are used in designing structures because they are one of the strongest ways to build.

Chapter 7: Circles

...ion to the Concepts of Circles

Circles can be found in many places in the environment. Circles have three things in common: they have a center or fixed point in the middle of the circle, every point on the circle is exactly the same distance from the center of the circle, and all points on the circle are on a single plane. Circles are named for the center point of the circle when they are labeled. Three non-collinear points generate a unique circle.

Concepts of Circles

1 Radius and Diameter

2 Circumference

3 Area

4 Chords, Tangents, and Secants

5 Arcs

6 Inscribed Angles

7 Finding the Equation of a Circle

Explanations of the Concepts of Circles

A **circle** is defined as the set of all points in a plane that are equidistant from a given point, called the **center** of the circle. Note that the center is not part of the circle. Points related to a circle can be inside the circle (**interior points**), outside the circle (**exterior points**), and points on the circle itself.

Examples of the regions of a circle:

A is an interior point.
B is a point on the circle.
C is an exterior point.

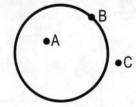

Chapter 7: Circles (cont.)

1 Radius and Diameter

The **radius** of a circle is a line segment that starts at the center of the circle and ends on the circle. Each radius of a given circle is exactly the same length, and there are many radii on a circle. The **diameter** of a circle is a line segment that passes through the center point and has both endpoints on the circle. All diameters in a single circle are equal.

Examples of circle, radius, and diameter:

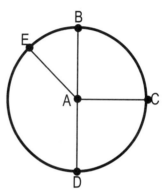

$\overline{AB}$, $\overline{AD}$, $\overline{AC}$, and $\overline{AE}$ are radii, and they are all equal.
$\overline{BD}$ is a diameter of circle A.

Notice that in the circle at the right, the diameter is twice as long as the radius. A formula for finding the diameter is $d = 2r$.

⊙A This symbol is read as "circle A."

2 Circumference

The circumference is the distance around the circle. Pi, represented by the symbol π, is determined by dividing the circumference of a circle by its diameter. **Pi** is the non-terminating and non-repeating decimal 3.141592 … The values 3.14 or $\frac{22}{7}$ are commonly used as the value of pi. You can find the circumference of a circle if you know the diameter of the circle. To find the circumference (C), find the diameter (d) and multiply the diameter by pi (π), or $C = \pi d$. The circumference of a circle can also be found by using the radius of the circle. Remember that the diameter is two times the radius. To find the circumference (C) with the radius (r), use $C = \pi 2r$.

Examples of finding the circumference:

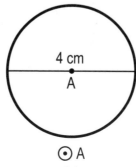

4 cm
A

⊙A

Chapter 7: Circles (cont.)

Problem: Find the diameter of Circle A: $d = 4$ cm

Step 1: Multiply the diameter by π.

$C = \pi d$ $\qquad\qquad\qquad$ $C = \pi d$

$C \approx 3.14(4)$ $\qquad\qquad$ $C \approx \frac{22}{7}(4)$

Answers: $C \approx 12.56$ $\qquad\qquad$ $C \approx \frac{88}{7}$

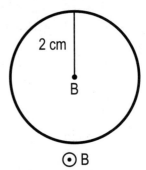

2 cm

B

Problem: Find the radius of Circle B: $r = 2$ cm. $\qquad$ ⊙ B

Step 1: Multiply 2 times the radius (which is equal to the diameter). Multiply by π.

$C = \pi 2r$ $\qquad\qquad\qquad$ $C = \pi 2r$

$C \approx 3.14(2)(2)$ $\qquad\qquad$ $C \approx \frac{22}{7}(2)(2)$

$C \approx 3.14(4)$ $\qquad\qquad$ $C \approx \frac{22}{7}(4)$

Answers: $C \approx 12.56$ $\qquad\qquad$ $C \approx \frac{88}{7}$

Circles A and B above are congruent circles because their diameters are equal. **Two theorems related to circles** are: two circles are congruent if, and only if, their diameters are the same length, and two circles are congruent if, and only if, their radii are the same length. That is, two circles are congruent if their radii or diameters are congruent.

❸ Area

The area of a circle is the area covered by the interior of the circle and the circle itself. The area of a circle (A) is found by multiplying pi (π) times the square of the radius (r^2) or $A = \pi r^2$. If the diameter is known instead of the radius, then area can be found by $A = \pi \left(\frac{d}{2}\right)^2$.

If you know the circumference, the area can be found by first finding the diameter of the circle, and then using $A = \pi \left(\frac{d}{2}\right)^2$. To find the diameter if you know the circumference, divide the circumference by pi because $C = \pi d$.

Chapter 7: Circles (cont.)

Examples of finding the area of a circle:

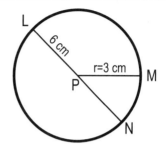

Problem:	Find the area of Circle P. Radius $\overline{PM}$ = 3 cm Diameter $\overline{LN}$ = 6 cm

If you know the radius:

$A = \pi r^2$

Step 1: $A \approx 3.14 \, (3^2)$

Step 2: $A \approx 3.14 \, (9)$

Answers: $A \approx 28.26$

If you know the diameter:

$A = \pi \left(\dfrac{d}{2}\right)^2$

$A \approx 3.14 \left(\dfrac{6}{2}\right)^2$

$A \approx 3.14 \, (9)$

$A \approx 28.26$

Circumference ≈ 18.85

If you know the circumference:

Step 1: Find the diameter: $18.85 = d\,(3.14)$ $= \dfrac{18.85}{3.14} = \dfrac{d(3.14)}{3.14}$

$d \approx 6$

Step 2: Find the area: $A = \pi \left(\dfrac{d}{2}\right)^2$

Step 3: $A \approx 3.14 \left(\dfrac{6}{2}\right)^2$

Step 4: $A \approx 3.14 \, (3)^2$

Step 5: $A \approx 3.14 \, (9)$

Answer: $A \approx 28.26$

Note that no matter which way the area was found, the area of circle P was always the same.

A **theorem on congruent circles** states that congruent circles have the same area. Also, if two circles have the same area or circumference, they must be congruent. This makes four ways to show that two circles are congruent. Two circles are congruent if: the radii are the same length, the diameters are the same length, the circumferences are the same, or the areas are the same.

Chapter 7: Circles (cont.)

 Chords, Tangents, and Secants

A **chord** of a circle is a line segment with endpoints on the circle. Chords are different from the radius and diameter because in a single circle, not all chords are always the same length. A chord does not have to pass through the center of a circle. Note that the diameter is a special chord that does pass through the center of a circle. The diameter of a circle is the **longest** chord in a circle.

Examples of the chords of a circle:

$\overline{EF}$ and $\overline{GH}$ are chords on Circle D.
$\overline{IJ}$ is a chord and is also a diameter.

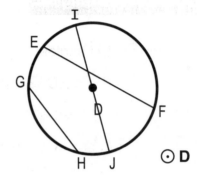

Other segments related to circles are tangents and secants. A **tangent** is a line that touches the circle in exactly one point. The point of intersection is called the **point of tangency**. A **secant line** for a circle is a line that intersects the circle in two points or contains a chord of the circle.

Examples of tangents:

Point of tangency of Line 1 is at point B.
Point of tangency of Line 2 is at point C.

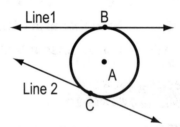

Theorems related to tangents include: if a line is tangent to a circle, then the tangent is perpendicular to the radius drawn to the point of tangency; conversely, if a line is perpendicular to the radius of a circle at its endpoint on the circle, then the line is tangent to the circle.

Examples of secants:

Secant Line 1 intersects the circle at points E and F.
Secant Line 2 intersects the circle at points C and D.

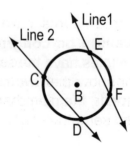

Chapter 7: Circles (cont.)

 Arcs

The number of degrees in a circle can be measured by measuring the central angles of a circle. **Central angles** are angles whose vertex is the center of the circle and whose sides intersect the circle.

Example of central angles:

Add all of the central angles:

m∠BAC + m∠BAD + m∠DAE + m∠EAC

90° + 75° + 15° + 180° = 360°

The number of degrees in a circle = 360°.

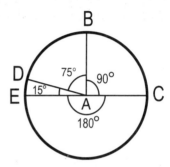

The full circle is 360°. Part of a circle is called an **arc**. A **semicircle** is an arc that is exactly half of a circle and is equal to 180°. Between any two points on a circle, there are two arcs. An arc that is smaller than a semicircle, or smaller than 180°, is a **minor arc**. A minor arc is labeled with two letters, for example, Arc AB, or written as $\overarc{AB}$. An arc larger than a semicircle, or more than 180°, is a **major arc**. We label major arcs with three letters, for example, Arc ABC, or written as $\overarc{ABC}$, to distinguish it from a minor arc.

Examples of arcs:

Arc EF is a minor arc because it is smaller than 180°.

Arc EDH is a major arc because it is larger than 180°.

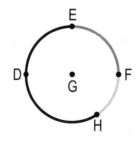

Congruent arcs have the same degree measure and the same length. In order to determine congruency, the arc needs to be measured. Arcs can be measured by measuring the central angle that is made when the radii intersect with the two endpoints of the arc. If the arc is a minor arc (less than 180°), the measure of the angle is the measure of the arc. If the arc is a major arc (greater than 180°), then subtract the measure of the minor arc from 360° to get the measure of the major arc.

Chapter 7: Circles (cont.)

Example of measuring a minor arc:

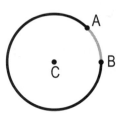

Problem: Measure Arc AB.

Step 1:   Draw in the radii to form a central angle.

Step 2:   Measure the central angle ACB.
 $\angle ACB = 45°$

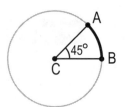

Answer: This is a minor arc, so the measure of
Arc AB is 45°.

Example of measuring a major arc:

Problem: Measure Arc CDE.

Step 1:   Draw in the radii to form a central angle.

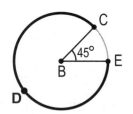

Step 2:   Measure the central angle CBE.
$\angle CBE = 45°$

Step 3:   Arc CDE is a major arc, so subtract the central
angle measurement from 360°.
$360° - 45 = 315°$

Answer: The measure of Arc CDE = 315°.

The **length of an arc** can be determined by using the circumference of the circle. First, find the circumference of the circle. Then divide the arc measurement by 360°, and multiply by the circumference of the circle.

Example of finding the length of the arc:

Problem: Find the length of Arc CD.

The measure of the Arc CD is 30°.

Diameter $\overline{AC} = 6$

Circumference = 6π

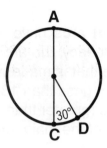

Chapter 7: Circles (cont.)

Step 1:   Find the circumference:

$$C = d\pi$$

$$C = 6(\pi)$$

Step 2:   Divide the measure of the arc by 360°:

$$\frac{30}{360} = \frac{1}{12}$$

Step 3:   Multiply the circumference (6π) times the quotient ($\frac{1}{12}$).

The length of Arc CD = $6\pi(\frac{1}{12})$.

Answer: The length of Arc CD = $\frac{1}{2}\pi \approx \frac{3.14}{2} = 1.57$

⑥   Inscribed Angles

An angle formed by two chords that have a common endpoint is called an **inscribed angle**. The arc that lies in the interior of the inscribed angle is called the **intercepted arc**.

Example of an inscribed angle:

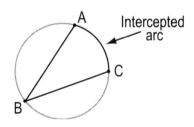

Arc AC is the intercepted arc.
Chords $\overline{AB}$ and $\overline{BC}$ form the inscribed angle.

The **measure of an inscribed angle** is half the measure of its intercepted arc. Find the measure of the intercept arc and divide it by two.

Chapter 7: Circles (cont.)

Example of finding the measure of an inscribed angle:

Problem: Find the measure of the inscribed angle ABC.

Step 1: Find the measure of the central angle.

Draw in the two radii to form the central angle.

Step 2: Measure the central angle ADC = 75°. This is a minor arc, so this is the measure of Arc AC.

Step 3: Divide the measure of the Arc AC by 2 = $\dfrac{75}{2}$ = 37.5

Answer: The measure of the inscribed angle is 37.5°.

7 Finding the Equation of a Circle:

Using a coordinate plane, you can find an algebraic equation for a circle. The standard equation of a circle with the radius r and the center (h, k) is $(x - h)^2 + (y - k)^2 = r^2$.

Examples of a circle in a coordinate plane:

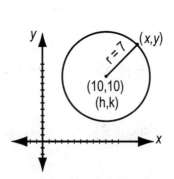

Problem: Find the algebraic equation for this circle.

Center is (10, 10)   Radius = 7

Step 1: Substitute the coordinates for the center of the circle into the formula:

$(x - h)^2 + (y - k)^2 = r^2$.

$(x - 10)^2 + (y - 10)^2 = 7^2$

Step 2: Simplify.

$(x - 10)^2 + (y - 10)^2 = 49$

Chapter 7: Circles (cont.)

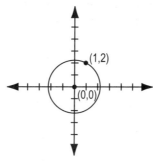

Problem: Write a standard equation for the circle.

The circle has a center at (0, 0).

A point on the circle is (1, 2).

Step 1:   Find the radius.

$(x - h)^2 + (y - k)^2 = r^2$

Substitute the center point and the point on the circle into the formula:

$(1 - 0)^2 + (2 - 0)^2 = r^2$

$(1)^2 + (2)^2 = r^2$

$1 + 4 = r^2$

$5 = r^2$

$\sqrt{5} = r$

Step 2:   The standard equation of this circle is:

$(x - 0)^2 + (y - 0)^2 = (\sqrt{5})^2$

Step 3:   Simplify.

$x^2 + y^2 = 5$

Name: _____ Date: _____

Chapter 7: Circles (cont.)

Practice: Circles

Directions: For questions 1–5, use circle P to identify which segments and lines are the radius, diameter, chord, tangents, and secants. There may be more than one answer for each question.

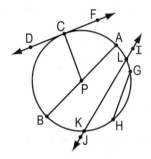

Radius, Diameter, Chord, Tangent, Secant

1. Radius or Radii: _____

    Explain why the segment(s) or line(s) you identified is/are the radius (radii).

    _____

2. Diameter(s): _____

    Explain why the segment(s) or line(s) you identified is/are the diameter(s).

    _____

3. Chord(s): _____

    Explain why the segment(s) or line(s) you identified is/are the chord(s).

    _____

4. Tangent(s): _____ Identify the Point of Tangency _____

    Explain why the segment(s) or line(s) you identified is/are the tangent(s).

    _____

5. Secant(s): _____

    Explain why the segment(s) or line(s) you identified is/are the secant(s).

    _____

Name: _____   Date: _____

 **Chapter 7: Circles (cont.)**

Circumference

Directions: Find the circumference of the circles in questions 6–7.

6. Circle A has a diameter of 8 cm. With a compass or string, tack, and pencil, draw the circle on your own paper.

   $C =$ _____

7. Circle B has a radius of 5 cm. With a compass or string, tack, and pencil, draw the circle on your own paper.

   $C =$ _____

Area

Directions: Find the area of the circles for questions 8–9.

8. Circle C has a diameter of 10 cm. With a compass or string, tack, and pencil, draw the circle on your own paper.

   $A =$ _____

9. Circle D has a radius of 7 cm. With a compass or string, tack, and pencil, draw the circle on your own paper.

   $A =$ _____

Central Angles

10. In Circle E, draw a central angle of 95°.

11. In Circle F, draw a central angle 35°.

Name: _____ Date: _____

Arcs

12. Find the measure of Arc HI in Circle G. Is this a major or minor arc? Why?

_____

_____

_____

_____

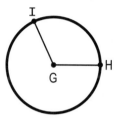

13. Find the measure of Arc GHE in Circle F. Is this a major or minor arc? Why?

_____

_____

_____

_____

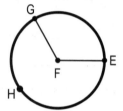

14. Find the length of Arc JK in Circle L. _____

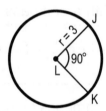

15. Find the measure of the inscribed angle PNO of Circle M. _____

Identify the intercept arc. _____

Identify the chords that form the inscribed angle. _____

Find the measure of the central angle. _____

Finding the standard equation of a circle

16. Graph the circle with the equation: $(x + 1)^2 + (y - 1)^2 = 9$

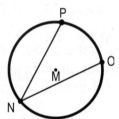

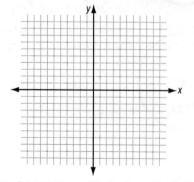

Name: _____   Date: _____

Chapter 7: Circles (cont.)

17. Write the equation for the circle below. _____

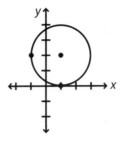

18. Find the center and radius of a circle with this equation: $(x - 3)^2 + (y + 4)^2 = 25$

_____

19. Write the equation for a circle with a center at (1, 3) and a radius of 4.

_____

20. Determine the center and radius of a circle with this equation: $(x - \frac{1}{2})^2 + (y + \frac{3}{4})^2 = \frac{1}{4}$

_____

21. Write the equation for a circle with the center of (-4, 0) and a radius of 2.

_____

Summary of Circles

A circle is a set of all points in a plane that are equidistant from a given point, called the center of the circle. Circles have three things in common: they have a center or fixed point in the middle of the circle, every point on the circle is exactly the same distance from the center of the circle, and all points on the circle are on a single plane. Points related to a circle can be inside the circle (interior points), outside the circle (exterior points), and points on the circle itself. The center of the circle is not a point on the circle.

The radius of a circle is a line segment with one endpoint at the center of the circle and the other endpoint on the circle. Each radius of a given circle is exactly the same length, and there are many radii on a circle. The diameter of a circle is a line segment that passes through the center point and has both endpoints on the circle. All diameters in a single circle are equal.

The circumference is the distance around the circle $C = d\pi$ or $C = 2r\pi$.

The area of a circle is the area covered by the interior and is found by $A = \pi r^2$ or $A = \pi(\frac{d}{2})^2$.

Chapter 7: Circles (cont.)

The chord of a circle is a line segment with endpoints on the circle. A diameter is a special chord, and it is the longest chord of a circle. A tangent is a line that touches the circle in exactly one point. The point of intersection is called the point of tangency. Secants are lines that intersect a circle in two points.

The amount of degrees in a circle can be measured by measuring the central angles of a circle. Central angles are angles whose vertex is the center of the circle and whose sides intersect the sides of the circle. The number of degrees in a circle = 360°.

Arcs can be measured by measuring the central angle that is made when the radii intersect with the two endpoints of the arc. If the arc is a minor arc (less than 180°), then the measure of the angle is the measure of the arc. If the arc is a major arc (greater than 180°), then subtract the measure of the minor arc from 360° to get the measure of the major arc.

An angle formed by two chords that have a common endpoint is called an inscribed angle. The arc that lies interior of the inscribed angle is called the intercept arc.

Using a coordinate plane, you can find an algebraic equation for a circle. The standard equation of a circle with the radius r and the center (h, k) is $(x - h)^2 + (y - k)^2 = r^2$.

Tips to Remember for Working With Circles

A circle is a special shape, and, as a result, it has many interesting properties and relationships. Be sure to remember the relationship between the radius and diameter, how to find the area and circumference given either the radius or diameter, and how to find either the radius or diameter if you know the area or circumference. Because the number of degrees in a circle is 360°, the measure of an arc on a circle is related to the measure of the central angle. This is similar to what happens on a clock when we see an angle made between the hour hand and minute hand. A formula for a circle can be written in algebraic form and shows the location of the center and the length of the radius.

Real Life Applications of Circles

As you look around, you will see that circles are found everywhere. Wheels, plates, tops of lampshades, tops of glasses, designs, and architecture are usually all examples of circles.

The properties of a circle are used when determining where to place the minute marks on a clock and when establishing time zones on the earth.

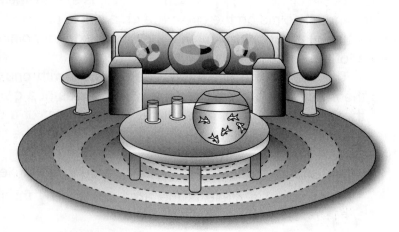

Answer Keys

Chapter 1: Introduction to Geometry: Practice (pages 20–22)

1. Answers will vary. One way to sort is by number of sides.
2. A, C
3. A, B
4, 5, 6. Answers may vary. Possible answers shown.

4.   5.   6.

7. Starting with a square piece of paper try to divide the paper into four squares, six squares, seven squares, eight squares, nine squares and ten squares. Not all the squares need to be congruent.

8. C
9. A. vertical   B. horizontal and vertical
10. The object without the pictures could have 120° rotational symmetry, but the designs are not the same on the arrows.

Chapter 2: Coordinate and Non-Coordinate Geometry: Practice (pages 33–36)

1. (6, 4) and (-2, 6)

$$\left(\frac{6 + (-2)}{2}, \frac{4 + 6}{2} \right)$$

$$\left(\frac{4}{2}, \frac{10}{2} \right) = (2, 5)$$

2. (-3, -3) and (5, 5)

$$\left(\frac{-3 + 5}{2}, \frac{-3 + 5}{2} \right)$$

$$\left(\frac{2}{2}, \frac{2}{2} \right) = (1, 1)$$

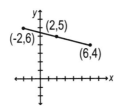

3. (3, -2) and (5, 12)

$$\left(\frac{3 + 5}{2}, \frac{-2 + 12}{2} \right)$$

$$\left(\frac{8}{2}, \frac{10}{2} \right) = (4, 5)$$

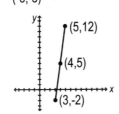

4. (2, 8) and (2, 3)

$$\left(\frac{2 + 2}{2}, \frac{8 + 3}{2} \right)$$

$$\left(\frac{4}{2}, \frac{11}{2} \right) = (2, 5.5)$$

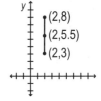

5. (3, 0) and (0, -2)

$$\frac{0 - (-2)}{3 - 0}$$

The slope is $\frac{2}{3}$

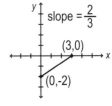

6. (-5, 1) and (5, -1)

$$\frac{1 - (-1)}{-5 - 5}$$

The slope is $-\frac{1}{5}$

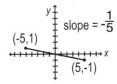

7. (0, 0) and (5, 3)

$$\frac{3 - 0}{5 - 0}$$

The slope is $\frac{3}{5}$

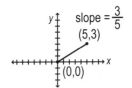

8. $\overleftrightarrow{AB}$ goes through A (-2, 1) and B (1, 2).

$$m = \frac{1 - 2}{-2 - 1} = \frac{-1}{-3} = \frac{1}{3}$$

$\overleftrightarrow{CD}$ goes through C (-1, 3) and D (0, 0).

$$m = \frac{3 - 0}{-1 - 0} = \frac{3}{-1} = -3$$

$\overleftrightarrow{AB}$ and $\overleftrightarrow{CD}$ are perpendicular; the slopes are negative reciprocals.

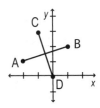

9. $\overleftrightarrow{EF}$ goes through E (-2, 1) ,and F (1, 2).

$$m = \frac{1 - 2}{-2 - 1} = \frac{-1}{-3} = \frac{1}{3}$$

$\overleftrightarrow{GH}$ goes through G (2, 1) and H (5, 2).

$$m = \frac{1 - 2}{2 - 5} = \frac{-1}{-3} = \frac{1}{3}$$

The lines are parallel; the slopes are equal.

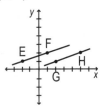

10. $\overleftrightarrow{IJ}$ goes through I (-2, 1) and J (1, 2).

$m = \dfrac{1-2}{-2-1} = \dfrac{-1}{-3} = \dfrac{1}{3}$

$\overleftrightarrow{KL}$ goes through K (-1, 2) and L (2, 3).

$m = \dfrac{2-3}{-1-2} = \dfrac{-1}{-3} = \dfrac{1}{3}$

The lines are parallel; the slopes are equal.

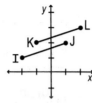

11. $5x - y + 2 = 0$

Change the equation into the y-intercept form $y = mx + b$.

$5x - y + 2 + y = 0 + y$

$y = 5x + 2$

The slope is $5 = \dfrac{5}{1}$ and the y-intercept is (0, 2).

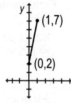

12. $4x + 2y = -8$

Change the equation into the y-intercept form $y = mx + b$

$4x - 4x + 2y = -8 - 4x$

$2y = -4x - 8$

$\dfrac{2y}{2} = \dfrac{-4x - 8}{2}$

$y = -2x - 4$

The slope is -2 and the y-intercept is (0, -4).

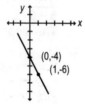

13. $y + 3 - 3x = 0$

Change the equation into the y-intercept form $y = mx + b$

$y + 3 - 3 - 3x + 3x = 0 - 3 + 3x$

$y = 3x - 3$

Slope is 3 and the y-intercept is (0, -3).

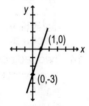

14. Slope = 2, Point (4, -4)

Substitute the point into the form $y = mx + b$ to find the y-intercept

$-4 = 2(4) + b$

Solve for b.

$-4 - 8 = 8 + b - 8$

$-12 = b$

The equation is $y = 2x - 12$.

15. Slope = $\dfrac{1}{2}$, Point (0, -1)

Substitute the point into the form $y = mx + b$ to find the y-intercept

$-1 = \dfrac{1}{2}(0) + b$

$-1 = b$

The equation is $y = \dfrac{1}{2}x - 1$.

16. (1, 1) and (6, 2)

Find the change by subtracting one pair of coordinates from the other.

Change in $y = 2 - 1 = 1$

Change in $x = 6 - 1 = 5$

Divide the change in y by the change in $x = \dfrac{1}{5}$

$\dfrac{5}{1}$ is the slope

Substitute the slope and one pair of coordinates and solve for b.

$y = mx + b$

$y = \dfrac{1}{5}x + b$

$1 = \dfrac{1}{5}(1) + b$

$1 = \dfrac{1}{5} + b$

$1 - \dfrac{1}{5} = \dfrac{1}{5} - \dfrac{1}{5} + b$

$\dfrac{4}{5} = b$

The equation is $y = \dfrac{1}{5}x + \dfrac{4}{5}$.

17. (0, 5) and (2, 0)

Find the change by subtracting one pair of coordinates from the other.

Change in $y = 5 - 0 = 5$

Change in $x = 0 - 2 = -2$

Divide the change in y by the change in $x = \dfrac{5}{-2} = -\dfrac{5}{2}$

$-\dfrac{5}{2}$ is the slope

Substitute the slope and one pair of coordinates and solve for b.

$y = mx + b$

$y = -\dfrac{5}{2}x + b$

$5 = -\dfrac{5}{2}(0) + b$

$5 = 0 + b$

$5 = b$

The equation is $y = -\dfrac{5}{2}x + 5$.

18. (3, -1) and (4, -2)

Find the change by subtracting one pair of coordinates from the other.

Change in $y = -1 - (-2) = 1$

Change in $x = 3 - 4 = -1$

Divide the change in y by the change in $x = \dfrac{1}{-1} = -\dfrac{1}{1}$

$-\dfrac{1}{1} = -1$ is the slope

Substitute the slope and one pair of coordinates and solve for *b*.

$y = mx + b$

$y = -1(x) + b$

$-1 = -1(3) + b$

$-1 = -3 + b$

$-1 + 3 = -3 + 3 + b$

$2 = 0 + b$

$2 = b$

The equation is $y = -1x + 2$.

19. (4, 2) and (1, 6)

$\sqrt{(x_2 - x_1)^2 + (y_2 - y_1)^2}$

$\sqrt{(4 - 1)^2 + (2 - 6)^2}$

$\sqrt{(3)^2 + (-4)^2}$

$\sqrt{9 + 16} = \sqrt{25} = 5$

20. (-3, 2) and (4, -1)

$\sqrt{(x_2 - x_1)^2 + (y_2 - y_1)^2}$

$\sqrt{(-3 - 4)^2 + (2 - (-1))^2}$

$\sqrt{(-7)^2 + (3)^2}$

$\sqrt{49 + 9} = \sqrt{58}$

Chapter 3: Angles: Practice (pages 49–51)

1. $m\angle = 90°$

2. $m\angle = 45°$

3. $m\angle = 110°$

4. $m\angle = 210°$

5. $m\angle = 15°$

6. Congruent angles are two angles that are exactly the same size and shape and have the same measure.
Drawings will vary. Check to see if they fit the definition.

7. Reflex angles are greater than 180° but less than 360°.
Drawings will vary. Check to see if they fit the definition.

8. Straight angles measure exactly 180°.
Drawings will vary. Check to see if they fit the definition.

9. Obtuse angles are more than 90° but less than 180°.
Drawings will vary. Check to see if they fit the definition.

10. Acute angles are less than 90°.
Drawings will vary. Check to see if they fit the definition.

11. Complementary angles are two angles that have a total measure of 90°.
Drawings will vary. Check to see if they fit the definition.

12. Supplementary angles are two angles that have a total measure of 180°.
Drawings will vary. Check to see if they fit the definition.

13. Vertical angles are formed when two lines intersect. These opposite angles always have the same measure.
Drawings will vary. Check to see if they fit the definition.

14. Two adjacent angles share a common side and a common vertex but do not share any interior points.
Drawings will vary. Check to see if they fit the definition.

15. An angle bisector is a ray that divides an angle into two equal parts.
Drawings will vary. Check to see if they fit the definition.

Chapter 4: Patterns and Reasoning: Practice (page 62)

1.

The answer above is based on the shading of the faces on the cube that goes: right, bottom, left, top, bottom, left, top, ... and is repetitive.

2. 0112358; This answer is based on the set of numbers shown earlier.

3. ∪∪ϽϚ∩∪∪ϽϚ∩∪∪

4. g   5. h   6. i   7. j
8. b   9. f   10. e   11. d
12. a   13. c

Chapter 5: Triangles: Practice (pages 77–79)

Match the triangle with its name and explain why it is that type of triangle.

1. b, c, d; All angles are less than 90°.
2. a; One angle is over 90°.
3. e; One angle is equal to 90°.
4. c; Two sides and two angles are congruent or equal.
5. b/d; All sides are equal.
6. d/b; All angles are equal.
7. a; No angles or sides are equal.
8. $s_1^2 + s_2^2 = h^2$
   $(5)^2 + (3)^2 = h^2$
   $25 + 9 = h^2$
   $\sqrt{34} = \sqrt{h^2}$
   $\sqrt{34} = h$
   $5.8 \approx h$ Note: this has been rounded to the nearest tenth.

9. $s_1^2 + s_2^2 = h^2$
   $s_1^2 + (5)^2 = 7^2$
   $s_1^2 + 25 = 49$
   $s_1^2 + 25 - 25 = 49 - 25$
   $s_1^2 = 24$
   $\sqrt{s_1^2} = \sqrt{24}$
   $s_1 = \sqrt{24}$
   $s_1 \approx 4.9$ cm Rounded to the nearest tenth.

10. Find the midpoint of $\overline{AC}$ and label the point D.
    Midpoint of $\overline{AC} = \left(\dfrac{x_1 + x_2}{2}, \dfrac{y_1 + y_2}{2}\right)$
    Midpoint of $\overline{AC} = \left(\dfrac{18 + (-2)}{2}, \dfrac{2 + 2}{2}\right)$
    Midpoint of $\overline{AC} = \left(\dfrac{16}{2}, \dfrac{4}{2}\right)$

    The coordinates of the perpendicular bisector are (8, 2).

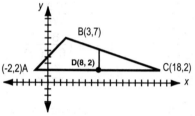

11. Half of 50 is 25; the bisector angle of angle ABC is 25°.

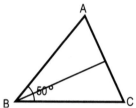

12. Midpoint of $\overline{DF} = \left(\dfrac{x_1 + x_2}{2}, \dfrac{y_1 + y_2}{2}\right)$
    Midpoint of $\overline{DF} = \left(\dfrac{-1 + 8}{2}, \dfrac{-1 + (-3)}{2}\right)$
    Midpoint of $\overline{DF} = \left(\dfrac{7}{2}, \dfrac{-4}{2}\right) = (3.5, -2)$

    The coordinates of the midpoint (G) of $\overline{DF}$ are (3.5, -2).
    Draw a line from the midpoint (G) to the vertex of ∠DEF.

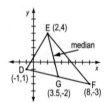

13. Find the altitude of the triangle NOP for ∠O.
    Using a protractor, draw a perpendicular from the vertex (O) of ∠NOP to $\overline{NP}$.

14. Show that the segment formed by midpoint J of $\overline{LM}$ and midpoint I of $\overline{KM}$ is parallel to $\overline{KL}$.

$$J = \left(\frac{x_1 + x_2}{2}, \frac{y_1 + y_2}{2}\right) \qquad I = \left(\frac{x_1 + x_2}{2}, \frac{y_1 + y_2}{2}\right)$$

$$J = \left(\frac{6 + 6}{2}, \frac{8 + (-1)}{2}\right) \qquad I = \left(\frac{-1 + 6}{2}, \frac{1 + (-1)}{2}\right)$$

$$J = \left(\frac{12}{2}, \frac{7}{2}\right) = (6, 3.5) \qquad I = \left(\frac{5}{2}, \frac{0}{2}\right) = (2.5, 0)$$

Find the slope of $\overline{IJ}$ and $\overline{KL}$.

$$\overline{IJ}\ m = \frac{rise}{run} = \frac{y_2 - y_1}{x_2 - x_1} \qquad \overline{KL}\ m = \frac{rise}{run} = \frac{y_2 - y_1}{x_2 - x_1}$$

$$\overline{IJ}\ m = \left(\frac{3.5 - 0}{6 - 2.5}\right) \qquad \overline{KL}\ m = \left(\frac{8 - 1}{6 - (-1)}\right)$$

$$\overline{IJ}\ m = \frac{3.5}{3.5} = \frac{1}{1} \qquad \overline{KL}\ m = \frac{7}{7} = \frac{1}{1}$$

The slopes are the same, so they are parallel.

15. $p = s_1 + s_2 + s_3$
    $p = 5 + 4 + 7$
    $p = 16$ cm

16. $p = s_1 + s_2 + s_3$
    $p = 4 + 15 + 9$
    $p = 28$ cm

17. $p = s_1 + s_2 + s_3$
    $p = 5.5 + 7.5 + 3$
    $p = 16$ cm

18. $A = \frac{1}{2}(bh)$
    $A = \frac{1}{2}(8 \times 5)$
    $A = \frac{1}{2}(40)$
    $A = 20$ cm²

19. $A = \frac{1}{2}(bh)$
    $A = \frac{1}{2}(10 \times 7)$
    $A = \frac{1}{2}(70)$
    $A = 35$ cm²

20. $A = \frac{1}{2}(bh)$
    $A = \frac{1}{2}(15 \times 4)$
    $A = \frac{1}{2}(60)$
    $A = 30$ cm²

Chapter 6: Polygons and Quadrilaterals: Practice (pages 94–95)

1. quadrilateral, rhombus, square, parallelogram, rectangle
2. octagon
3. triangle (equilateral)
4. quadrilateral, rectangle, parallelogram
5. pentagon
6. triangle (isosceles)
7. convex
8. concave or non-convex
9. equilateral, equiangular, regular
10. equiangular
11. equilateral, equiangular, regular
12. equilateral
13. octagons are in 10, 11, and 12.
14. Draw a regular quadrilateral.

15. Draw an equilateral hexagon that is not equiangular. Answers will vary. Two examples are shown.

 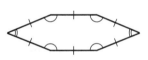

16. Let x be the measure of the smallest angle. Then $x + 20°$, $x + 40°$, $x + 60°$, and $x + 80°$ are the measures of the other four angles. Knowing that the sum of the angles of a pentagon is 540°, we can write the equation: $x + (x + 20°) + (x + 40°) + (x + 60°) + (x + 80°) = 540°$

$$5x + 200° = 540°$$
$$5x + 200° - 200° = 540° - 200°$$
$$5x = 340°$$
$$\frac{5x}{5} = \frac{340°}{5}$$
$$x = 68°$$

So 68°, 88°, 108°, 128°, and 148° are the measures of the angles.

17. Find m∠A.
    The sum of the interior angles of a quadrilateral is 360°.

    m∠A = 360° − 96° − 112° − 42°

    m∠A = 110°
18. 6 sides/hexagon
19. 5 sides/pentagon
20. 8 sides/octagon

21. 108°
22. 135°
23. 90°

Chapter 7: Circles: Practice (pages 108–111)

1. Radius or Radii: $\overline{PA}$, $\overline{PC}$, $\overline{PB}$
   They all start at the center of the circle and end on the edge of the circle.
2. Diameter(s): $\overline{BA}$
   It is a line segment that goes through the center and has two endpoints on the edges of the circle.
3. Chord(s): $\overline{BA}$, $\overline{GH}$, $\overline{KL}$
   Line segments that intersect the circle twice.
4. Tangent(s): $\overleftrightarrow{DF}$
   Point of Tangency: C
   A tangent is a line that intersects the circle in exactly one point.
5. Secant(s): $\overleftrightarrow{JI}$
   It is a line that intersects the circle in two places.

For questions 6–9, teacher check circles.

6. $C = d\pi$ $C = d\pi$
   $C = 8\pi$ $C = 8\pi$
   $C \approx 8(3.14)$ OR $C \approx 8(\frac{22}{7})$
   $C \approx 25.12$ $C \approx \frac{176}{7}$ cm

7. $C = 2\pi r$ $C = 2\pi r$
   $C = 2(5)\pi$ $C = 2(5)\pi$
   $C \approx 10(3.14)$ OR $C \approx 10(\frac{22}{7})$
   $C \approx 31.4$ cm $C \approx \frac{220}{7}$ cm

8. $A = \pi(\frac{d}{2})^2$ $A = \pi(\frac{d}{2})^2$
   $A = \pi(\frac{10}{2})^2$ $A = \pi(\frac{10}{2})^2$
   $A = \pi(5)^2$ $A = \pi(5)^2$
   $A = \pi(25)$ $A = \pi(25)$
   $A \approx 3.14(25)$ OR $A \approx \frac{22}{7}(25)$
   $A \approx 78.5$ cm² $A \approx \frac{550}{7}$ cm²

9. $A = \pi(r)^2$ $A = \pi(r)^2$
   $A = \pi(7)^2$ $A = \pi(7)^2$
   $A = \pi(49)$ $A = \pi(49)$
   $A \approx 3.14(49)$ OR $A \approx \frac{22}{7}(49)$
   $A \approx 153.86$ cm² $A \approx 154$ cm²

For questions 10–11, teacher check central angles.

10. Location of the angle may vary but the angle should be 95°, and the segments should start in the center and end on the edge of the circle.
11. Location of the angle may vary but angle should be 35°, and the segments should start in the center and end on the edge of the circle.

For questions 12–15, teacher check arcs.

12. $\angle IGH = 115°$; It is a minor arc because it is less than 180°, so the measure of the Arc HI = 115°.
13. Arc GHE = 240°; It is a major arc because it is more than 180°. The measure of the minor arc is 120°, so the measure of the Arc GHE = 360° − 120° = 240°.
14. Circumference ≈ 18.84
    Measure of angle JLK = 90°
    Divide 90° by 360° and multiply by circumference.
    $\frac{90}{360} = 0.25$
    0.25(18.84) = 4.71   Length of Arc JK = 4.71.

15. Intercept Arc: PO
    Chords that form the inscribed angle: $\overline{NP}$ and $\overline{NO}$
    Central angle PMO = 74°. This is a minor arc, so this is the measure of Arc PO = 74°.
    Find the measure of the inscribed angle: divide the measure of the Arc PO by 2. 74 ÷ 2 = 37, so the measure of the inscribed angle is 37°.

16. Radius = 3
    Center = (-1, 1)

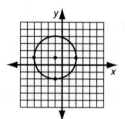

17. $(x - 1)^2 + (y - 2)^2 = 2^2$
    $(x - 1)^2 + (y - 2)^2 = 4$

18. Center (3, -4)
    Radius = 5

19. $(x - 1)^2 + (y - 3)^2 = 4^2$
    $(x - 1)^2 + (y - 3)^2 = 16$

20. Center = $(\frac{1}{2}, -\frac{3}{4})$
    Radius = $\frac{1}{2}$

21. $(x + 4)^2 + (y - 0)^2 = 2^2$
    $(x + 4)^2 + y^2 = 4$

References

Brown, R., Dolciani, M., Sorgenfrey, R., Cole, W., (1997). *Algebra Structure and Method Book 1.* Evanston, IL: McDougal Littell.

Chicago Mathematics Project. *Connected Mathematics.* University of Chicago. Found online at: http://www.math.msu.edu/cmp/curriculum/algebra.htm

Edwards, E. (1990). *Algebra for Everyone.* Reston, VA: National Council of Teachers of Mathematics.

Freudenthal Institute at the University of Utrecht/University of Wisconsin / NSF. *Math in Context.* http://showmecenter.missouri.edu/showme/mic.shtml

Larson, R., Boswell, L., Stiff, L. (1998) *Geometry and Integrated Approach.* Evanston. IL: McDougal Littell.

Long, L. (2001). *Painless Geometry.* Hauppauge, NY: Barron's Educational Series.

National Council of Teachers of Mathematics. (2000). *Principles and standards for school mathematics.* Reston, VA: National Council of Teachers of Mathematics.

National Council of Teachers of Mathematics (NCTM). (2004). *Standards and expectations for algebra.* Reston, VA: National Council of Teachers of Mathematics. Found online at: http://www.nctm.org

Web Resources

About Math
> http://math.about.com/

A History of Pi
> http://www-groups.dcs.st-and.ac.uk/~history/HistTopics/PI_through_the_ages.html

Annenburg CPB – Shape and Space in Geometry
> http://www.learner.org/teacherslab/math/geometry/

Ask Dr. Math
> http://forum.swarthmore.edu/dr.math/

Binary Numbers
> http://www.math.grin.edu/~rebelsky/Courses/152/97F/Readings/student-binary.html

Boxer Math
> http://www.boxermath.com

Color Math Pink
> http://www.colormathpink.com

References (cont.)

Condensed Matter Physics – Quasicrystals
    http://www.cmp.catech.edu/~lifshitz/symmetry.html

Cool Math Sites
    http://www.cte.jhu.edu/techacademy/web/2000/heal/mathsites.htm

Dave's Math Tables
    http://www.sisweb.com

Designer Factions
    http://www.math.rice.edu/~lanius/Patterns/design2.html

Ed Helper.com
    http://www.edhelper.com/algebra.htm

Fascinating Folds
    http://www.education.gov.lc/mathjocv/html%20file/origami/Welcome%20to%20Fascinating%20
    folds

Figures and Polygons – Math League
    http://www.mathleague.com/help/geometry/polygons.htm

Four Types of Symmetry
    http://www.mathforum.org/sum95suzanne/symsusan.html

Gallery of Interactive Geometry
    http://www.geom.uiuc.edu/apps/gallery/html

Geometric Junkyard
    http://www.ics.uci.edu/~eppstein/junkyard/topic.html

Geometry Junkyard – Symmetry
    http://www.ics.uci.edu/~eppstein/junkyard/sym.html

Geometry Online
    http://www.math.rice.edu/~lanius/Geom/

Getting to Know Shapes
    http://www.illuminations.nctm.org/index_d.aspx?id=406

History of Quilt Patterns
    http://www.womenfolk.com/quilt_pattern_history/patternlinks.htm

Holt, Rinehart, and Winston Mathematics in Context
    http://www.hrw.com/math/mathincontext/index.htm

References (cont.)

Honey Bee Facts
http://www.honey.com/kids/facts.html

Interactive Mathematic Miscellany and Puzzles
http://www.cut-the-knot.org/algebra.shtml

Line Symmetry
http://www.adrianbruce.com/Symmetry/

Math Archives: Topics in Mathematics
http://www.archives.math.utk.edu/topics/

Math for Morons Like Us
http://www.library.thinkquest.org/20991/geo/index.html

Math Forum
http://www.forum.swarthmore.edu/

Math Forum – Geometry/Shapes 1, 2, 3 Dimensions/Vectors
http://www.mathforum.org/library/view/2650.html

Mega Mathematics
http://www.c3.lanl.ov/mega-math/

Miss Glosser's Math Goodies
http://www.mathgoodies.com

Oldest Escher Collection on the Web
http://www.comcast.net/~davemc0/Escher/

Ole Miss: Problems of the Week
http://www.olemmiss.edumathed/problem.htm

Patterns Possibilities
http://www.cte.jhu.edu/techacademy/web/2000/heal/rsrchist.htm

PBS Teacher Source – Geometry and Shapes
http://www..pbs.org/teachersource/recommended/mathlk_geometry.shtm

Purple Math
http://www.purplemath.com/modules/solvrtnl.htm

Reflectional Symmetry
http://www..geom.uiuc.edu/~demo5337/s97a/reflect.html

Regular Polyhedra or Platonic Solids
http://www.enchantedlearning.com/math/geometry/solids/

References (cont.)

Reichman, H. and Kohn, M.(2004) Math Made Easy.
    Found online at: http://www.mathmadeeasy.com/

Rotational Symmetry
    http://www.geom.uiuc.edu/~demo5337/s97a/reflect.html

Science Behind Snowflakes
    http://www.msnbc.msn.com/id/3077345/#BODY

Science U – Geometry - Symmetry
    http://www.scienceu.com/geometry/articles/tiling/symmetry.html

Science U Geometry Center
    http://www.scienceu.com/geometry/

Show Me Center
    http://www.shoemecenter.missouri.edu/showme/

Snowflakes
    http://www.snowflakebentley.com/

SOS Mathematics
    http://www.sosmath.com/

Surfing the Net With Kids
    http://www.surfnetkids.com/

Symmetry and Patterns of Oriental Rugs
    http://www.mathforum.org/geometry/rugs/

Symmetry and the Shape of Space
    http://www.comp.uark.edu/~strauss/symmetry.unit/index.html

The Mathematical Art of M.C. Escher
    http://www.mathacademy.com/pr/minitext/escher/

Think Quest Geometry
    http://www.library.thinkquest.org/2647/geometry/geometry.htm

Totally Tessellations
    http://www.thinkquest.org/library/site_sum.html?16661&url=16661/escher.html

Translational Symmetry
    http://www.geom.uiuc.edu/~demo5337/s97a/translate.html

Two-Dimensional Shapes and Line Symmetry
    http://www.adrianbruce.com/Symmetry/9.htm

References (cont.)

University of Akron Theoretical and Applied Mathematics
http://www.math.uakron.edu~dpstory/mpt_home.html

Wikipedia – Symmetry
http://www.en.wikipedia.org/wiki/Symmetry

World's Top Websites on Symmetry
http://www.dirs.org/wiki-article-tab.cfm/symmetry

Real Life Applications of Math

Applied Academics: Applications of Mathematics – Careers
http://www.bced.gov.bc.ca/careers/aa/lessons/math.htm

Exactly How Is Math Used in Technology?
http://www.math.bcit.ca/examples/index.shtml

Geometry in Action
http://www.ics.uci.edu/~eppstein/geom.html

Line Symmetry
http://www.adrianbruce.com/Symmetry/

Mathematics Association of America – Careers
http://www.maa.org/careers/index.html

NASA Space Link
http://www.spacelink.msfc.nasa.gov/index.html

Recreational Math
http://www.ics.edu/~eppstein/recmath.html

Teacher Notes

MONDAY: _____

_____

_____

_____

TUESDAY: _____

_____

_____

_____

WEDNESDAY: _____

_____

_____

_____

THURSDAY: _____

_____

_____

_____

FRIDAY: _____

_____

_____

_____